Word Pronunciation

BY
DEBORAH WHITE BROADWATER

COPYRIGHT © 2001 Mark Twain Media, Inc.

ISBN 1-58037-163-9

Printing No. CD-1384

Mark Twain Media, Inc., Publishers
Distributed by Carson-Dellosa Publishing Company, Inc.

Table of Contents

WORD Pronunciation

Introduction

It is important to know how to pronounce words correctly. This will help you with spelling and with writing. Many spelling mistakes are corrected when you learn how to pronounce a word. It is easier to spell words if you work on saying them clearly and correctly.

A good place to learn the correct pronunciation of a word is in the dictionary. The pronunciation is usually shown after the entry word. Sometimes it is in parentheses and sometimes it is just written after the entry word.

A word is respelled for pronunciation purposes. It usually looks different than the correct spelling of the word. There are marks and letters that are changed. Some words have upside-down letters. Words that have more than one syllable are divided and have marks at the syllables. These are all clues to help you learn to pronounce the word correctly.

Dictionaries have a short pronunciation key at the end of each page and a longer and more complete pronunciation key in the front.

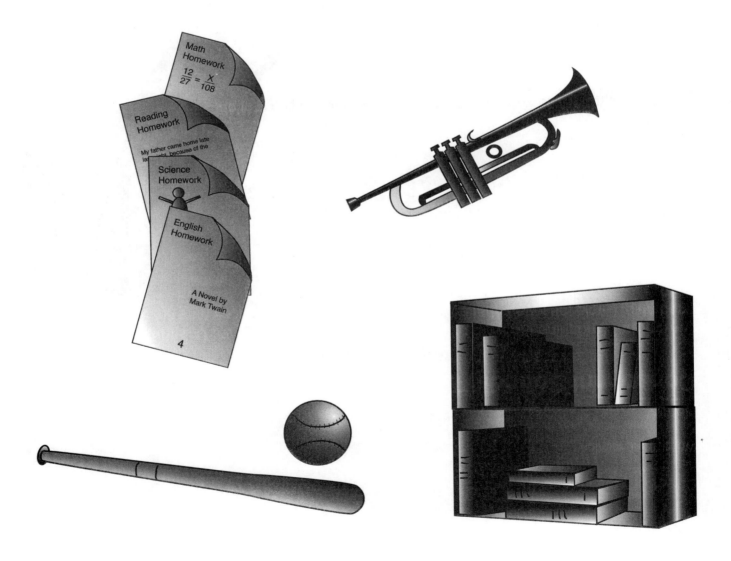

Short Vowels: *Introduction*

WORD Pronunciation

The short vowel sounds are:

a - as in hat

e - as in bed

i - as in sit

o - as in hot

u - as in cup

Short vowel sounds are shown in the dictionary in two ways.

Unmarked - dog \dog\

Marked - dog (dŏg)

The symbol to mark a short vowel sound (˘) is called a **breve**.

census - sĕn′ səs

indent - ĭn dĕnt′

In this book, short vowels will be unmarked.

Short Vowels: *Exercise 1*

Name: _____ Date: _____

WORD Pronunciation

Directions: Complete the following sentences with words that have the short vowel sound \a\. Use the dictionary if you need help.

disaster	cafeteria	flash	admit	space	facts
stay	matador	ask	appetite	example	perhaps
sad	subtract	salad	table	active	saddle

1. We cannot _____ you to the game without a ticket.

2. I saw a _____ of light when the picture was taken.

3. The _____ held the cape in front of the bull.

4. The horse needs to stand still while you put the _____ on it.

5. After raking leaves all day, I had a hearty _____.

6. My mother is _____ in the school PTA.

7. It was a _____ when the wrong chemicals were mixed together.

8. I buy my lunch in the school _____.

9. Did you _____ your dad if you may go to the movies with us?

10. Mrs. Weed put an _____ of the problem on the board.

11. We were to list _____ about George Washington for the test.

12. _____ we could use the gym for our basketball tournament.

13. The boy looked very _____ when his ice cream spilled.

14. We learned to add and _____ in math class.

15. My mom is going to make a _____ for dinner.

Short Vowels: *Exercise 2*

WORD Pronunciation

Directions: Look at the dictionary pronunciation of the word. Circle the short \a\ sound on the dictionary spelling in red. Write the correct spelling of the word on the blank. Circle the short \a\ sound on the correct spelling in red. Use the word in a sentence.

1. ak sel′ ə rāt′   _____

   _____

2. mid′ af′ tər no͞on′   _____

   _____

3. kap′ chər   _____

   _____

4. van′ ə tē   _____

   _____

5. fash′ ən   _____

   _____

6. lam′ ə nāt′   _____

   _____

7. val′ ən tīn′   _____

   _____

8. san′ dəl   _____

   _____

4

Name: _____ Date: _____

Short Vowels: *Exercise 3* WORD Pronunciation

Directions: Complete the following sentences with words that have the short vowel sound \e\.
Use the dictionary if you need help.

sentences	bench	less	leap	closet	letter
hundred	keep	check	open	neck	left
established	below	tennis	forget	definitions	met

1. The students _____ on the tennis courts after school.

2. My mother wants to put a _____ in the garden.

3. I have to clean out the _____ in my bedroom.

4. We had six _____ of words to learn for our history quiz.

5. Jeff hurt his _____ when his football helmet came off in the game.

6. I think there is _____ in my glass than in Bill's.

7. My hands are full; could you please _____ the door for me?

8. The mailman should deliver the _____ to my house today.

9. Mrs. Abbott took her _____ to the bank yesterday.

10. The student council was hoping to sell one _____ tickets to the dance.

11. Do you put the fork on the _____ or the right side of the plate when you set the table?

12. What year was the Jamestown colony _____?

13. I seldom _____ to do my homework.

14. How long have you been taking _____ lessons?

15. I'll write the first four _____ and you write the last four.

Name: _____ Date: _____

Short Vowels: *Exercise 4* WORD Pronunciation

Directions: Look at the dictionary pronunciation of the word. Circle the short \e\ sound on the dictionary spelling in red. Write the correct spelling of the word on the blank. Circle the short \e\ sound on the correct spelling in red. Use the word in a sentence.

1. rez′ ər vwär′   _____

_____

2. ə tach′ ment   _____

_____

3. sel′ fish   _____

_____

4. prə pel′ ənt   _____

_____

5. jen′ ū ən   _____

_____

6. fen′ əl   _____

_____

7. en′ ər jīz′   _____

_____

8. fē es′ tə   _____

_____

Name: _____   Date: _____

Short Vowels: *Exercise 5*   WORD Pronunciation

Directions: Complete the following sentences with words that have the short vowel sound \i\.
Use the dictionary if you need help.

fit	switch	picture	beautiful	active	fish
pine	drift	different	dime	drilled	live
gigantic	trip	sling	slippery	admit	punishment

1. The passenger train had to _____ from one track to another when the freight train passed.

2. Sally asked for a _____ book to read.

3. Dad _____ the holes in the board, and I put in the pegs.

4. The fish are very _____ in the tank when it is time for feeding.

5. The waves at the beach _____ in and out with the tide.

6. Whose _____ is that on the wall in the classroom?

7. Beth bought a _____ dress for her brother's wedding.

8. Carol, do you _____ on Hampshire Street?

9. My cat, Tigger, sits by the aquarium and watches the _____.

10. To the small child the horse seemed _____.

11. Did your mom give you a _____ for coming home late from the movie?

12. The roads were very _____ after the ice storm.

13. Be careful that you don't _____ over toys on the playroom floor.

14. I will _____ that I was the one who ate all of the chocolate cake.

15. How many people do you think we can _____ in the car?

Name: _____ Date: _____

Short Vowels: *Exercise 6*

WORD Pronunciation

Directions: Look at the dictionary pronunciation of the word. Circle the short \i\ sound on the dictionary spelling in red. Write the correct spelling of the word on the blank. Circle the short \i\ sound on the correct spelling in red. Use the word in a sentence.

1. fig′ yər _____

   _____

2. ath let′ ik _____

   _____

3. dis ā′ bəl _____

   _____

4. krit′ i kəl _____

   _____

5. rōō′ mə tiz′ əm _____

   _____

6. mis′ chif _____

   _____

7. brij′ ing _____

   _____

8. nik′ əl _____

   _____

Name: _____ Date: _____

Short Vowels: *Exercise 7*   WORD Pronunciation

Directions: Complete the following sentences with words that have the short vowel sound \o\. Use the dictionary if you need help.

chopped	geology	common	open	cone	soccer
binoculars	jukebox	shown	robber	crocodile	dog's
pond	plot	improper	compactor	anybody	monogrammed

1. My _____ name is Rusty.

2. We usually know flowers by the _____ name.

3. The bank _____ stole $1000 from the local bank.

4. I really liked the _____ of the movie we saw last night.

5. We put quarters in the _____ and picked some tunes for it to play.

6. It is _____ to keep your hat on when you are inside a building.

7. _____ is the study of the earth and rocks and minerals.

8. When Matt and Bill were at the zoo they saw a _____.

9. Taylor and Jordan joined the _____ team this year.

10. Mike helped his mom dig and fill a _____ in the backyard this year.

11. When we go to the baseball game, I like to take the _____.

12. Did _____ understand last night's math homework?

13. Kevin would like a trash _____ so he doesn't have to take out the trash.

14. Beverly wanted a sweater with her initials _____ on it.

15. My dad and brother _____ wood for our fireplace.

Name:_____ Date:_____

Short Vowels: *Exercise 8*

WORD Pronunciation

Directions: Look at the dictionary pronunciation of the word. Circle the short \o\ sound on the dictionary spelling in red. Write the correct spelling of the word on the blank. Circle the short \o\ sound on the correct spelling in red. Use the word in a sentence.

1. op′ ə rā′ tər   _____

_____

2. fond′ nis   _____

_____

3. chop′ stiks′   _____

_____

4. kot′ ij   _____

_____

5. bod′ ē   _____

_____

6. spot′ lis   _____

_____

7. bot′ n ē   _____

_____

8. kom′ pakt′   _____

_____

Short Vowels: *Exercise 9*

WORD Pronunciation

Directions: Complete the following sentences with words that have the short vowel sound \u\. Use the dictionary if you need help.

summer	supper	pulse	huge	brush	sunrise
puppet	tube	chuckled	fluttered	crunches	hunter
industries	sculptor	blushed	cucumber	run	quite

1. In the morning I sometimes forget to _____ my hair.

2. The _____ made a statue for the park.

3. Mom is fixing hamburgers and french fries for _____.

4. Our cat wants us to think that he is a great _____ of mice.

5. When Mrs. James complimented Sue, she _____.

6. While I was in the garden, a butterfly _____ by me.

7. Chen and Lul need to be at the bus stop almost before _____.

8. Liz grew _____ vines in the middle of her garden.

9. After jogging, Dad checks his _____.

10. Mrs. Stevens and Mrs. Vogel are going to put on a _____ show after school.

11. School has just started, and I am ready for _____.

12. How far do you think you can _____ in one minute?

13. In gym class we had to do ten _____ and six pull-ups.

14. Our town is looking for new _____ to build here.

15. Mr. White _____ when he heard the joke.

Name: _____ Date: _____

Short Vowels: *Exercise 10*

WORD Pronunciation

Directions: Look at the dictionary pronunciation of the word. Circle the short \u\ sound on the dictionary spelling in red. Write the correct spelling of the word on the blank. Circle the short \u\ sound on the correct spelling in red. Use the word in a sentence.

1. kul′ tə vāt′ _____

   _____

2. but′ n _____

   _____

3. en gulf′ _____

   _____

4. guz′ əl _____

   _____

5. in dus′ trē əs _____

   _____

6. blunt _____

   _____

7. in jus′ tis _____

   _____

8. tun′ əl _____

   _____

Name: _____   Date: _____

Short Vowels: *Exercise 11*

WORD Pronunciation

Directions: In each of the following sentences, circle the words with short vowel sounds.

1. How long have you lived in Quincy, Illinois?

2. Carol asked to go on the picnic with them.

3. Barbara is going to the store with her dad.

4. I would like to have cake for my birthday.

5. Taylor and Jordan asked Allison to go to the movies with them.

6. Is milk a good thing to drink at lunchtime?

7. Whose book is that on the table?

8. I think there were six pencils in the box when I opened it.

9. Tim will bring Matt and Kim to the celebration.

10. What kind of dog do you have?

11. Can you play soccer tonight?

12. I think I have to dry the dishes after dinner today.

13. Mrs. Li is helping us write stories about our lives.

14. This is really a difficult assignment.

15. Please close the window when you leave.

Name: _____ Date: _____

Short Vowels: *Exercise 12*

WORD Pronunciation

Directions: Use your dictionary to write the pronunciation of each of the following words. Circle the letters that are the short vowel sounds.

1. enthusiastic _____

2. penguin _____

3. apprenticeship _____

4. cafeteria _____

5. trustee _____

6. swiftly _____

7. canyon _____

8. brush _____

9. conference _____

10. implant _____

11. granite _____

12. wrap _____

13. unfortunate _____

14. twenty _____

15. shellac _____

Short Vowels: *Exercise 13*

WORD **Pronunciation**

Directions: Use your dictionary to write the pronunciation of each of the following words. Circle the letters that are the short vowel sounds.

1. playpen _____

2. capture _____

3. debate _____

4. follow _____

5. ballistic _____

6. lessor _____

7. wand _____

8. felt _____

9. astonished _____

10. lingo _____

11. pocket _____

12. vast _____

13. yellow _____

14. nimble _____

15. erector _____

Long Vowels: *Introduction*

The long vowel sounds are:

a - as in cake

e - as in eat

i - as in ice

o - as in oath

u - as in human

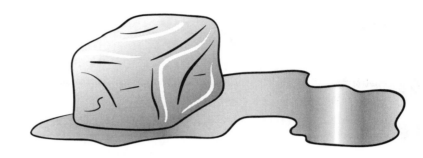

Long vowel sounds are shown in the dictionary with a straight line over the vowel.

mean - mēn

The symbol to mark a long vowel sound (¯) is called a macron.

overseas - ō′ vər sēz′   prepay - prē pā′

Long vowel sounds can be spelled several ways.

- The long sound \ā\ is found in words like *cake* - a-consonant-e; it is also found in words like *aim* - ai, or it is also found in words like *hay* - ay, or words like *neighbor* - eigh. The pronunciation in the dictionary will have the long ā mark.
- The long sound \ē\ is found in words like *week* -ee; it is also found in words like *mean* - ea and in words like *pretty* - y. Some special spellings of the e sound are found in words like *shield* - ie or *seize* - ei-consonant-e or *believe* - ie-consonant-e.
- The long \ī\ is found in words like *hide* - i-consonant-e; it is also found in words like *high* - igh; it is also found in words like *mind* - i or in words like *sky* - y.
- The long sound \ō\ is found in words like *both* - o or found in words like *vote* - o-consonant-e. It can be found in words like *boat* - oa, and it can be found in words like *row* - ow or words like *dough* - ough.
- The long sound \ū\ is found in words like *humid* - u or in words like *rule* - u-consonant-e. The sound can also be found in words like *rue* - ue.
  Note: In some dictionaries, long ū is written yo͞o.
       mutual - mū′ chü əl   or   mutual - myo͞o′ cho͞o əl
  This book will use ū to represent the long ū sound.

It is important when you see a word that you think may have a long vowel sound to check the pronunciation. There are many ways long vowels may be written.

16

Long Vowels: *Exercise 1*

Name: _____   Date: _____

WORD Pronunciation

Directions: Complete the following sentences with words that have the long vowel sound \a\. Use the dictionary if you need help.

details	praise	batter	bake	play	weighs
ants	eighth	frail	highway	vacancies	cable
betray	stadium	candid	layer	incorporate	tame

1. My mom and dad took us to a _____ at the auditorium.

2. We are trying to _____ some songs into our class project.

3. The truck drove on the _____ overpass.

4. Keshia received a lot of _____ from Mrs. Rivera for her history report.

5. The hotel didn't have any _____.

6. At what temperature should we _____ the brownies?

7. The _____ from the computer was tangled with the monitor cord.

8. Our Airedale dog _____ seventy-five pounds.

9. Carol and Steve went to the ballgame at the _____.

10. When you share a secret, you _____ a confidence.

11. Mario tried to _____ a wild rabbit.

12. What do you think school will be like in the _____ grade?

13. After being ill for several weeks, Chris became very _____.

14. I would like a three-_____ cake for my birthday.

15. Mrs. Hagan told us to put _____ in our narrative essays.

Long Vowels: *Exercise 2*

Directions: Look at the dictionary pronunciation of the word. Circle the long \a\ sound on the dictionary spelling in red. Write the correct spelling of the word on the blank. Circle the long \a\ sound on the correct spelling in red. Use the word in a sentence.

1. ôl′ tər nāt′   _____

  _____

2. kō ôrd′ 'n ā′ shən   _____

  _____

3. fā′ vər   _____

  _____

4. dāz   _____

  _____

5. pōst′ nāt′ 'l   _____

  _____

6. fā′ ling   _____

  _____

7. ə kā′ zhən   _____

  _____

8. rek′ rē ā′ shən   _____

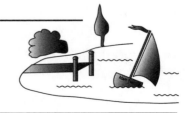

  _____

         18

Name: _____   Date: _____

Long Vowels: *Exercise 3*   WORD Pronunciation

Directions: Complete the following sentences with words that have the long vowel sound \e\. Use the dictionary if you need help.

chimney	believe	referee	went	retrieve	peacocks
vehicles	leotards	obvious	seized	medium	field
receive	suggest	eager	scream	special	decompose

1. Our dog likes to run and _____ a ball.

2. Carri's ballet class will wear _____ for the dance recital.

3. Latoya asked for a _____-sized sweatshirt for her birthday.

4. We have a corn _____ in our neighborhood.

5. Mr. Meyer thought the answer to the math problem should be _____.

6. Our zoo is going to get three _____ next spring.

7. When Dad built the fire in the fireplace, the smoke didn't go up the _____.

8. Stephanie was _____ for the race to begin.

9. The basketball player _____ the ball and shot the winning basket.

10. Do you think newspapers will _____ in the landfill?

11. Who is going to _____ our volleyball game?

12. It is great fun to ride roller coasters and _____.

13. What grade did Elena _____ on her speech in English?

14. Do all _____ have wheels?

15. I _____ it may snow tomorrow night.

Name:_____ Date:_____

Long Vowels: *Exercise 4*

WORD Pronunciation

Directions: Look at the dictionary pronunciation of the word. Circle the long \e\ sound on the dictionary spelling in red. Write the correct spelling of the word on the blank. Circle the long \e\ sound on the correct spelling in red. Use the word in a sentence.

1. ôrd′ dn âr′ ə lē _____

_____

2. bi lēf′ _____

_____

3. är′ chə rē _____

_____

4. bēst _____

_____

5. ster′ ē ə fon′ ik _____

_____

6. skrēm _____

_____

7. ri sēv′ _____

_____

8. kē′ hōl′ _____

_____

Name: _____   Date: _____

Long Vowels: *Exercise 5*   WORD Pronunciation

Directions: In the following sentences, circle all the words with long vowel sounds.

1. I need to get a medium-sized sweatshirt.

2. Did your dog eat all of her food?

3. I saw Jane and Kevin at the race.

4. Did you have cake and ice cream at your party?

5. Tyler and Phil are going to play football next year.

6. I have finished my homework for tomorrow.

7. When did Blake and Liz say they were going to come over?

8. Todd and Carmen are playing chess right now.

9. I wonder if we will get much snow this winter.

10. The storm brought three inches of rain.

11. Did you get the answers to numbers five and eight?

12. My mother grows flowers in our yard.

13. Amy needs to finish her science project.

14. Where did you put the green and blue paper?

15. This is the last day to finish the assignment.

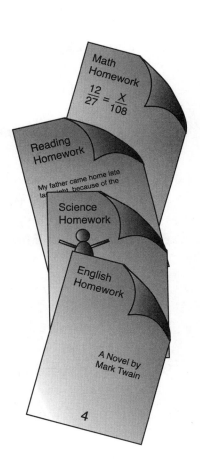

21

Name: _____ Date: _____

Long Vowels: *Exercise 6*   WORD Pronunciation

Directions: Complete the following sentences with words that have the long vowel sound \i\. Use the dictionary if you need help.

strike	pride	ice	pine	high	sky
wind	five	sitter	reply	limp	cider
final	identical	might	incident	license	unify

1. My house is the one with the big _____ tree in the front yard.

2. Adam took _____ in the fact that he had won his tennis tournament.

3. Be careful when you _____ the old grandfather clock.

4. It is difficult for some countries to _____ after being separate for many years.

5. My sister will be _____ when I am twelve.

6. Fall is a great time to drink hot apple _____.

7. How _____ is Mount McKinley?

8. The pitcher tried to _____ out the home run hitter.

9. Taylor and Jordan are _____ twins.

10. We pushed the wagon with all our _____ and it moved just an inch.

11. Look at that hot air balloon in the _____.

12. You have to be sixteen in our state to get your driver's _____.

13. Mrs. Hernandez said that she would grade our _____ projects soon.

14. Ben sent a _____ to Jamal's e-mail on the school computer.

15. On a hot day it is good to have _____ in your lemonade.

Name: _____ Date: _____

Long Vowels: *Exercise 7*

WORD Pronunciation

Directions: Look at the dictionary pronunciation of the word. Circle the long \i\ sound on the dictionary spelling in red. Write the correct spelling of the word on the blank. Circle the long \i\ sound on the correct spelling in red. Use the word in a sentence.

1. pīp   _____

   _____

2. tīt′ l   _____

   _____

3. ri lī′ ə bəl   _____

   _____

4. jī′ rāt   _____

   _____

5. ū′ nə fī′   _____

   _____

6. siv′ ə līz′   _____

   _____

7. bī munth′ lē   _____

   _____

8. klīm   _____

   _____

Name: _____ Date: _____

Long Vowels: *Exercise 8*

WORD Pronunciation

Directions: Complete the following sentences with words that have the long vowel sound \o\. Use the dictionary if you need help.

notice	trombone	hot	vote	both	oath
zoology	widow	crocodile	note	swallowed	slopes
show	toast	float	popular	antisocial	follow

1. Did your boat _____ when you sailed it in the lake?

2. My brother David plays the _____ in the school band.

3. Heather and Ming are going to ski on the _____ in Colorado.

4. Will _____ Hal and Debbie go on the trip to Washington, D.C.?

5. Mrs. Brown took the _____ that Janice wrote in class.

6. Sometimes Jim is so _____ he won't join any school clubs.

7. Matt is studying _____ at Purdue University.

8. Luis will _____ the class how to do the next math problem.

9. Did you _____ on the schedule where the next football game will be played?

10. Mrs. Chen told us to make sure we _____ the directions at the top of the paper.

11. To be president you must take the _____ of office.

12. I like _____ for breakfast and my dad likes cereal.

13. I tried to get the button away from the dog before she _____ it.

14. Mrs. Stevens' husband died, so she is a _____.

15. It is important to make sure you _____ in all elections.

Name:_____ Date:_____

Long Vowels: *Exercise 9*

WORD Pronunciation

Directions: Look at the dictionary pronunciation of the word. Circle the long \o\ sound on the dictionary spelling in red. Write the correct spelling of the word on the blank. Circle the long \o\ sound on the correct spelling in red. Use the word in a sentence.

1. trans pōz′   _____

   _____

2. swol′ ō   _____

   _____

3. tûr′ bō jet′   _____

   _____

4. dē kōd′   _____

   _____

5. di spōz′   _____

   _____

6. drōn   _____

   _____

7. ô′ dē ō vizh′ ū əl   _____

   _____

8. bī fō′ kəl   _____

   _____

25

Name: _____ Date: _____

Long Vowels: *Exercise 10*

WORD Pronunciation

Directions: Complete the following sentences with words that have the long vowel sound \u\. Use the dictionary if you need help.

solitude	dude	fuel	duck	university	mutual
cucumbers	tube	gratitude	summer	continued	discontinued
dispute	unicycles	trumpet	humid	utensil	united

1. What kind of _____ does an airplane use?

2. Mrs. White showed her _____ to the children by baking brownies.

3. I don't know if John and Stephen can settle their _____ over who owns the bike.

4. Our garden was overflowing with _____ this year.

5. Will your sister go to the state _____ next year?

6. The clowns in the circus were riding _____ in the center ring.

7. By _____ agreement, the baseball game was stopped when it got dark.

8. In the summer, St. Louis is very _____.

9. The toy company _____ making wooden puzzles because they did not sell.

10. It is nice to go to the _____ of the library and read a book.

11. With the basketball team _____, they were able to win the championship.

12. Leon _____ his writing assignment in class the next day.

13. It is hard to remember which _____ goes on which side of the plate.

14. My dog chewed the end of my _____ of toothpaste.

15. My family is going to a _____ ranch for our vacation.

Name:_____ Date:_____

Long Vowels: *Exercise 11*

WORD Pronunciation

Directions: Look at the dictionary pronunciation of the word. Circle the long \u\ sound on the dictionary spelling in red. Write the correct spelling of the word on the blank. Circle the long \u\ sound on the correct spelling in red. Use the word in a sentence.

1. tūb   _____

_____

2. ū ten′ səl   _____

_____

3. jen′ ū in   _____

_____

4. mū′ chü əl   _____

_____

5. nū′ səns   _____

_____

6. stū′ dē ō′   _____

_____

7. ū′ nə fī′   _____

_____

8. bär′ bə kū′   _____

_____

Name: _____ Date: _____

Long Vowels: *Exercise 12*   WORD Pronunciation

Directions: Use your dictionary to write the pronunciation of each of the following words. Circle the letters that are the long vowel sounds.

1. subzero   _____

2. social   _____

3. appeal   _____

4. studio   _____

5. gratify   _____

6. impolite   _____

7. daze   _____

8. eagerness   _____

9. peacock   _____

10. pint   _____

11. nineteen   _____

12. keyhole   _____

13. painter   _____

14. leotard   _____

15. streetcar _____

28

Long Vowels: *Exercise 13*

WORD Pronunciation

Directions: Use your dictionary to write the pronunciation of each of the following words. Circle the letters that are the long vowel sounds.

1. connive _____

2. tunic _____

3. mold _____

4. gainer _____

5. bayberry _____

6. sky _____

7. freak _____

8. biology _____

9. transpose _____

10. maiden _____

11. deepen _____

12. supervise _____

13. overflow _____

14. postdate _____

15. enlighten _____

Name: _____   Date: _____

Short and Long Vowels Review: *Crossword Puzzle*

Directions: Write the correct spelling of each dictionary pronunciation below in the crossword puzzle.

ACROSS

2. in spekt′
4. od
5. lak
7. līf′ gärd′
11. ē′ kwəl
13. ī′ lənd
14. mär′ bəl
16. del′ i kit
17. līt
18. mod′ ə fī′

DOWN

1. fel
3. tə dā′
6. kôst′ lē
8. jen′ ər əl
9. di liv′ ə rē
10. lā′ zē
12. en fōld′
14. mid′ tûrm
15. ri fûr′
19. ok′ yə pī′

30

Name: _____ Date: _____

Short and Long Vowels Review: *Word Search* WORD Pronunciation

Directions: Write the correct spelling of the word on the line following the dictionary spelling. Then search for the word in the word search.

1. gān   _____

2. not   _____

3. ri mōov′   _____

4. tempt   _____

5. jug′ əl   _____

6. den′ əm   _____

7. ō′ shən   _____

8. fō′ nē   _____

9. hok′ ē   _____

10. jel′ ə tən   _____

11. bit′ ər   _____

12. di pres′   _____

```
H W I J I O O O Q O Q C A C J N A O D I
K E P C Y P S K L V S I I A R I P W F T
F K N O T I E H I S M C Q L W T B Z X G
U B F Q D N M W P A D E N I M A T H S R
F T B Y K I A G H B E X H S V L X I Q B
X Q F M Y B K I C O S J Q E C E D S X D
X H W O Q I F Y B Q C R D Q O G R Q K Y
W R V H E T D T X D S K Q Y O A J E B T
E P L A V T S N W M T I E R N R H L Y K
J M V T T E H R S Q E J O Y A R M G R H
Z E X X O R D C B S X B L T E T D G S A
T T T Y D K I S A C E Y K H C X B U T M
R P W I E G W G S Z T R T G O T O J C Q
W X M Q S N H K G S W H P M J Z Y Y T X
K B G E M Q O Q D E O P B E S D S S S A
Z H N T T V B H R A B B S Y D A T L K D
I O H U H U N O P N U K G A I N C S X C
V X X I G N M N K T I E N D P J B P J Y
A D T X E V O M E R S A Z E M F K P H F
P V E H C Z U E R P O U A X J W H M I W
```

Consonant Sounds: *Introduction Part 1* WORD Pronunciation

There are many consonant sounds. Some are made with one consonant and some are made with two consonants. Some consonants are called hard and some are called soft, depending on the sound that they make.

It is important to practice making the consonant sounds and using the dictionary to help with pronunciation.

\b\ - is a consonant sound. You hear it in words like *back* and *tab.*

\d\ - is a consonant sound. You hear it in words like *do* and *bad.*

\f\ - is a consonant sound. You hear it in words like *fly* and *snuff.*

\g\ - is a consonant sound. You hear it in words like *good* and *big.*

\h\ - is a consonant sound. You hear it in words like *hit* and *behind.*

\l\ - is a consonant sound. You hear it in words like *lemon* and *yellow.*

\m\ - is a consonant sound. You hear it in words like *magic* and *him.*

\n\ - is a consonant sound. You hear it in words like *never* and *done.*

\p\ - is a consonant sound. You hear it in words like *potato* and *popper.*

\s\ - is a consonant sound. You hear it in words like *sun* and *pass.*

\t\ - is a consonant sound. You hear it in words like *ton* and *potter.*

\v\ - is a consonant sound. You hear it in words like *victor* and *river.*

\w\ - is a consonant sound. You hear it in words like *wonder* and *away.*

Name: _____ Date: _____

Consonant Sounds: *Exercise 1* WORD Pronunciation

Directions: Underline the words that have the consonant sound \b\. Use the dictionary if you need help. Circle the letters that spell the \b\ sound. Some sentences may have more than one word.

1. We have a large birch tree in our backyard.

2. I brought hamburger buns to the barbecue.

3. My sister and brother both play the tuba in the school band.

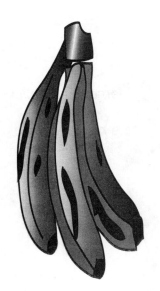

4. There was a subtle brown mark on the yellow banana.

5. A dog and a rabbit are warm-blooded animals.

6. In New York many people ride the subway to work and school.

7. If you are absent from school, you need to make up your assignments.

8. The temperatures in Minnesota are often in the subzero range.

9. Beth blushed when she won the Best Essay Award.

10. Student Council is having a banquet for the retiring teachers.

11. We trimmed the bushes and put the twigs in large bags.

12. Mrs. Lopez is bilingual; she speaks both Spanish and English.

13. Ben had mosquito bites all over his body.

14. Mrs. Douglas is always looking for the first robin of spring.

15. I missed my bus this morning and had to walk to school.

Consonant Sounds: *Exercise 2* WORD Pronunciation

Name: _____ Date: _____

Directions: Underline the words that have the consonant sound \d\. Use the dictionary if you need help. Circle the letters that spell the \d\ sound. Some sentences may have more than one word.

1. I think the dog is underneath the front porch.

2. The directions said to describe your favorite ice cream cone.

3. The address goes on the front of the envelope.

4. Mrs. Gates said, "Put down your pencils and paper and listen."

5. The weather today looks very dreary.

6. In our school we get our grades mid-year.

7. It is my job to dust the furniture in our house.

8. What does a cooper make?

9. That dime had a dull finish on it.

10. Would you please put the ladder back in the garage today?

11. Mrs. Tate is a widow; her husband died last year.

12. In children's stories, fairies live under toadstools.

13. To take the picture of the sunset, I needed a tripod on which to set my camera.

14. On our trip last summer we stopped at a roadside park to eat our lunch.

15. It is difficult to deal with rude people.

Name: _____ Date: _____

Consonant Sounds: *Exercise 3* WORD Pronunciation

Directions: Underline the words that have the consonant sound \f\ as in *fish.* Use the dictionary if you need help. Circle the letters that spell the \f\ sound. Some sentences may have more than one word.

1.   Michael has always wanted to learn to fly an airplane.

2.   Three feathers floated down from the sky.

3.   Our science teacher showed us several types of fungus in science class.

4.   Jeff realized it is hard to say farewell to good friends.

5.   My father and I rake leaves in the fall.

6.   When Lauren fell off her bike, she fractured her leg.

7.   Grandmother's powder puff was on her vanity table.

8.   You can tell how fresh a tomato is by the firmness.

9.   In Mexico, May 5 is a fiesta day.

10.   My fluffy sweater has little fuzz balls on it.

11.   There was a long line at the drinking fountain, so Frances decided to wait.

12.   Liz was not certain of the formula for the area of a circle.

13.   Tanya bumped her forehead on the frame of the car door.

14.   The faculty at Park Elementary School is planning a family night.

15.   Do we need forty or fifty leaf specimens for the science fair?

Name: _____ Date: _____

Consonant Sounds: *Exercise 4* WORD Pronunciation

Directions: Underline the words that have the consonant sound \g\ as in *gab*. Use the dictionary if you need help. Circle the letters that spell the \g\ sound. Some sentences may have more than one word.

1. My sister got a gardenia corsage for the dance.

2. Our science class went to the granite quarry to see how the rock had been formed.

3. Brad's guardian signs all of his permission slips for field trips.

4. The sunshine on the lake made the water glisten.

5. Mrs. Garcia warned the students not to gossip about others.

6. I wish I could get the flowers in my garden to grow as well as Mr. White's.

7. The ball hit the ground in the outfield and rolled to the gate.

8. I need to get a ticket to travel to Ghana.

Airline Ticket
Flight # 224
To GHANA

9. Curt had to grip the gross-looking frog to keep it from slipping away.

10. Michelle liked the green jacket better than the gray one.

11. My grandpa calls a record player a gramophone.

12. General Grant fought in the Civil War.

13. Mrs. Phillips thinks grammar is a very important school subject.

14. Gregory and Karen have to clean out the gutters on Saturday.

15. People say this old house is haunted by ghosts.

Name: _____ Date: _____

Consonant Sounds: *Exercise 5* WORD Pronunciation

Directions: Underline the words that have the consonant sound \h\. Use the dictionary if you need help. Circle the letters that spell the \h\ sound. Some sentences may have more than one word.

1. Mr. Meyers is my hero.

2. Wouldn't it be nice to have eyesight like a hawk?

3. Hard-boiled eggs are easy to cut in quarters or halves.

4. Carri put the hats and coats on the hooks behind the door.

5. I think the hens and rooster are hiding in the chicken coop.

6. Mrs. Harris is going to her high school reunion.

7. Maria had a hedgehog named Shermie.

8. Dominic hauled the cans to the recycling station.

9. Please hurry and put the hot rolls on the table for dinner.

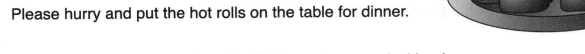

10. When I woke up this morning, the fields were covered with a haze.

11. Haley fell headfirst down the stairs.

12. It is important to take care of your heart so you can stay healthy.

13. It is important to study history and your heritage.

14. The Garretts hired horses to take them down the Grand Canyon.

15. We had a worksheet to study homonyms at home.

Name: _____ Date: _____

Consonant Sounds: *Exercise 6* WORD Pronunciation

Directions: Underline the words that have the consonant sound \l\. Use the dictionary if you need help. Circle the letters that spell the \l\ sound. Some sentences may have more than one word.

1. Brian wants to follow in his father's footsteps and become a lawyer.

2. It is nice to have candles or a lantern when the lights go out.

3. Is the front door locked?

4. The lazy boy would not get the ladder for his father.

5. I can't decide between the lavender notebook or the yellow one.

6. Becky lacked the right color of pencil to finish her poster.

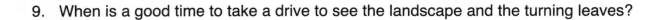

7. The lunar surface looked like it had many craters in it.

8. I think my lemonade is lukewarm instead of cold.

9. When is a good time to take a drive to see the landscape and the turning leaves?

10. Do you eat lunch right at noon, or do you eat earlier?

11. I let my piano lesson time slip my mind.

12. Alex couldn't get enough leverage to move the large box.

13. Which has less population, Latvia or Lithuania?

14. I must take a list with me to the grocery store.

15. Our dog had a litter of cute little puppies.

38

Name: _____ Date: _____

Consonant Sounds: *Exercise 7* WORD Pronunciation

Directions: Underline the words that have the consonant sound \m\. Use the dictionary if you need help. Circle the letters that spell the \m\ sound. Some sentences may have more than one word.

1. We have six members in our family, not counting the dog.

2. Wednesday is considered midweek.

3. Lindsey likes to read mystery books.

4. This summer the Franz family is going to Munich, Germany.

5. The musicians in the orchestra played songs from Broadway musicals.

6. Mrs. Smith modified the math assignment.

7. Jason and Monica have a mutual friend who lives in Minneapolis, Minnesota.

8. I think the minimum amount of work in school will not be enough.

9. Jamie was really good at mimicking the sounds of animals.

10. "Is mercury still put in thermometers?" asked Miriam.

11. Madam and monsieur are two French words.

12. The magician came to the party to do magic tricks.

13. There are several mountain ranges in America.

14. Do you subscribe to any magazines?

15. I would like to have my monogram put on a sweater.

Name: _____ Date: _____

Consonant Sounds: *Exercise 8* WORD Pronunciation

Directions: Underline the words that have the consonant sound \n\. Use the dictionary if you need help. Circle the letters that spell the \n\ sound. Some sentences may have more than one word.

1. There were numerous books to choose from at the book fair.

2. Kevin never did answer Ms. Toft's question about worms.

3. Pat had a noticeable spot on the front of his shirt.

4. Enrique had three nickels, two dimes, and nine quarters.

5. Student Council needs to find a service project to work on.

6. Sean's little sister is a nuisance.

7. Ben needs to be home by nightfall.

8. The Cardinals' pitcher pitched a no-hitter game in the World Series.

9. Gold miners were always looking for large gold nuggets.

10. Linda's sister is nineteen years old.

11. Did you give your dog a name, or will it be nameless?

12. My favorite dinner is noodles with broccoli and chicken.

13. This project requires both narrow and wide ribbon.

14. Many nations have presidents as the head of office.

15. Did you notify Mr. Grayson that you were running for class office?

Name: _____ Date: _____

Consonant Sounds: *Exercise 9* WORD Pronunciation

Directions: Underline the words that have the consonant sound \p\. Use the dictionary if you need help. Circle the letters that spell the \p\ sound. Some sentences may have more than one word.

1. Every morning we say the Pledge of Allegiance.

2. When I was in Panama, I saw a peacock on a patio.

3. My papa told me that he wore patches on his old pants.

4. What proof do you need to show that I am the owner of the pen?

5. It's Andrea's turn to mop the kitchen floor.

6. Juan's presentation for science was almost perfect.

7. Mike's Boy Scout project was a puppet stage for the school.

8. Do you like pumpkin pie or pudding?

9. Nathan had to pack his suitcase for his trip to Pennsylvania.

10. The little sparrow was perched on the telephone pole.

11. It's fun to pop popcorn and watch movies on television.

12. A postscript is a little extra written at the bottom of a letter.

13. I believe it's two pints to a quart, not two quarts to a pint.

14. Will you preserve the cucumbers and make pickles?

15. The panel is going to go on the wall to cover the posters.

Name: _____ Date: _____

Consonant Sounds: *Exercise 10* WORD Pronunciation

Directions: Underline the words that have the consonant sound \s\ as in *saw*. Use the dictionary if you need help. Circle the letters that spell the \s\ sound. Some sentences may have more than one word.

1. James wore sandals to the sandy beach.

2. A squirrel scampered across the sidewalk.

3. You must be self-confident to stand in front of the whole school and give a speech.

4. There is much smog in San Francisco, California.

5. The failed science experiment left a smell in the classroom.

6. The selfish little girl would not share the toys.

7. Samantha can spike the ball over the volleyball net.

8. The pep squad had a rally to raise school spirit.

9. I don't remember if I put a stamp on the letter or not.

10. Did you say you needed the stapler or staple remover?

11. After all the exercise, I am going to need a substantial lunch.

12. Kyoko always wears such stylish clothes.

13. What strange things did that baby bird just swallow?

14. Baseball players chew sunflower seeds.

15. My brother got a new suit to wear to the wedding.

Name: _____ Date: _____

Consonant Sounds: *Exercise 11* WORD Pronunciation

Directions: Underline the words that have the consonant sound \t\ as in *top.* Use the dictionary if you need help. Circle the letters that spell the \t\ sound. Some sentences may have more than one word.

1. The little toothless turtle crossed the street.

2. Our school is getting grants to buy things for technology.

3. The tomatoes in the bag are rotten.

4. My mom transplanted a tree from the front yard to the back yard.

5. Glendale School won the trophy for the soccer tournament.

6. The treasurer of the council said we had no money.

7. The farmer was tending his fields.

8. How many time zones are there in the world?

9. Mary took six tulips and some greenery and made a flower arrangement.

10. Are you having toast for breakfast, or cereal?

11. Mike thought his meat was too tough to cut.

12. My mother will not let me get a tattoo.

13. There is a small tear in the old tablecloth.

14. A tornado warning is in effect until midnight.

15. We used tortillas to make tacos.

Name: _____ Date: _____

Consonant Sounds: *Exercise 12* WORD Pronunciation

Directions: Underline the words that have the consonant sound \v\. Use the dictionary if you need help. Circle the letters that spell the \v\ sound. Some sentences may have more than one word.

1. Sometimes we vary the route we walk home from school.

2. There was a vacancy at the hotel where we wanted to stay.

3. My grandma said she takes various vitamins.

4. The weather vane on the house also shows the wind direction.

5. Does that store sell a variety of products?

6. Our class visited a violinist who plays in the symphony orchestra.

7. The space vehicles were left on the moon.

8. Lewis likes vanilla ice cream.

9. The veterans will be having a parade on November 11.

10. Is your dog vicious, or is it tame?

11. When you make pickles, you need to have vinegar to put in the jars.

12. The President has the power to veto bills.

13. Explorers took voyages to search for the new world.

14. Beth wanted her mom to make her a velvet dress.

15. I don't like to venture outside on very cold days.

Name: _____ Date: _____

Consonant Sounds: *Exercise 13* WORD Pronunciation

Directions: Underline the words that have the consonant sound \w\ as in *win*. Use the dictionary if you need help. Circle the letters that spell the \w\ sound. Some sentences may have more than one word.

1. Did you try to grow watermelons in your garden?

2. I lost my wallet when I was out walking yesterday.

3. Paul can't watch television on weeknights.

4. Abby would like a warm sweater for Christmas.

5. There are six walnut trees in our backyard.

6. Marco wants good weather for the baseball game.

7. Do you wear the same thing in winter as you do in summer?

8. Steven always has a wrapped sandwich for his lunch.

9. The wind blew so hard the airport windsock was blowing straight out from the pole.

10. In fairy tales, the fairy godmother has a magic wand to grant wishes.

11. Would you like to be a woodcarver when you grow up?

12. The pioneers traveled westward in covered wagons.

13. The toddler tried to wiggle out of his mother's arms.

14. The old chair legs were wobbly.

15. I walked through a spider web on the way to school today.

Name: _____ Date: _____

Consonant Sounds: *Exercise 14* WORD Pronunciation

Directions: Use your dictionary to write the pronunciation of each of the following words. Circle the letters that make consonant sounds \b\, \d\, \f\, \g\, \h\, \l\, \m\, \n\, \p\, \s\, \t\, \v\, and \w\.

1. pretend _____

2. overboard _____

3. mistake _____

4. admire _____

5. weeknight _____

6. departure _____

7. castle _____

8. wiggle _____

9. ultimate _____

10. quarter _____

11. scenic _____

12. purpose _____

13. suggest _____

14. comprehend _____

15. automation _____

46

Name: _____ Date: _____

Consonant Sounds: *Exercise 15* WORD Pronunciation

Directions: Use your dictionary to write the pronunciation of each of the following words. Circle the letters that make consonant sounds \b\, \d\, \f\, \g\, \h\, \l\, \m\, \n\, \p\, \s\, \t\, \v\, and \w\.

1. announcer   _____

2. seize   _____

3. dreadful   _____

4. unhappy   _____

5. wonderful   _____

6. truant   _____

7. grant   _____

8. football   _____

9. peace   _____

10. believable   _____

11. copper   _____

12. umbrella   _____

13. animal   _____

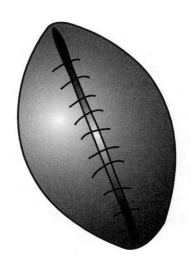

47

Name: _____ Date: _____

Consonant Sounds: *Exercise 16* WORD Pronunciation

Directions: Look at the dictionary pronunciation of each word. Circle the consonant sounds \b\, \d\, \f\, \g\, \h\, \l\, \m\, \n\, \p\, \s\, \t\, \v\, and \w\ on the dictionary spelling in red. Write the correct spelling of the word on the blank. Circle the consonant sounds on the correct spelling in red. Use the word in a sentence.

1. dok   _____

_____

2. pis′ tən   _____

_____

3. ed′ it   _____

_____

4. kōs′ təl   _____

_____

5. sal′ əd   _____

_____

6. tī′ gər   _____

_____

7. mī′ nər   _____

_____

8. pə tā′ tō   _____

_____

Name: _____ Date: _____

Consonant Sounds: *Exercise 17* WORD Pronunciation

Directions: Look at the dictionary pronunciation of each word. Circle the consonant sounds \b\, \d\, \f\, \g\, \h\, \l\, \m\, \n\, \p\, \s\, \t\, \v\, and \w\ on the dictionary spelling in red. Write the correct spelling of the word on the blank. Circle the consonant sounds on the correct spelling in red. Use the word in a sentence.

1. plump _____

_____

2. man′ dāt′ _____

_____

3. ôr′ dər _____

_____

4. nīt′ lē _____

_____

5. sôr′ ing _____

_____

6. hôlt _____

_____

7. nok _____

_____

_____

8. grāp _____

_____

_____

Name: _____ **Date:** _____

Consonant Sounds: *Exercise 18* WORD Pronunciation

Directions: Look at the dictionary pronunciation of each word. Circle the consonant sounds \b\, \d\, \f\, \g\, \h\, \l\, \m\, \n\, \p\, \s\, \t\, \v\, and \w\ on the dictionary spelling in red. Write the correct spelling of the word on the blank. Circle the consonant sounds on the correct spelling in red. Use the word in a sentence.

1. kā′ bəl　　_____

　　_____

2. pig′ ē　　_____

　　_____

3. grā′ vē　　_____

　　_____

4. tōt′ ′l　　_____

　　_____

5. nos′ trəl　　_____

　　_____

6. peg′ bôrd′　　_____

　　_____

7. skruf　　_____

　　_____

8. bob′ kat′　　_____

　　_____

Consonant Sounds: *Introduction Part 2* WORD Pronunciation

Some consonants make more than one sound.

\j\ - is a consonant sound. It is made with the letter "j" as in *just.* It is also made with a "g" as in *magic* and "dg" as in *fudge.* This is called the soft \g\ sound.

\k\ - is a consonant sound. It is made with the letter "k" as in *keep.* It is also made with the letter "c" as in *scold,* the letter combination "ck" as in *clock,* or the letter combination "ch" as in *chorus.*

\c\ is a consonant, but doesn't have a sound of its own. When "c" comes at the beginning of a word, it makes a hard \c\ sound like a \k\ or the soft \c\ sound like an \s\. When "c" is followed by "e," "i," or "y," it makes a soft \c\ or \s\ sound. When "c" is followed by "o," "a," or "u," it makes the hard \c\ or \k\ sound.

\z\ - is a consonant sound. You hear it in words like *zoo.* The \z\ sound is also made with an "s" as in *please* and *these.*

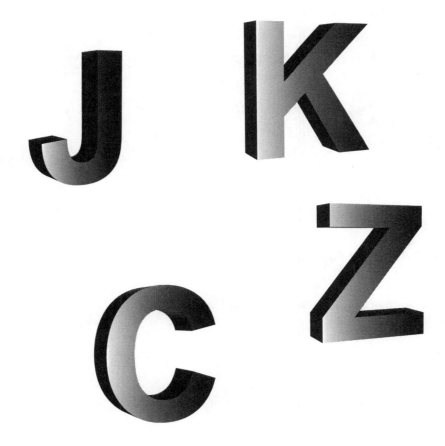

Name:_____ Date:_____

Consonant Sounds: *Exercise 19* WORD Pronunciation

Directions: Underline the words that have the consonant sound \j\ as in *just* or *magic.* Use the dictionary if you need help. Circle the letters that spell the \j\ sound. Some sentences may have more than one word.

1. We got to see the giraffe at the zoo.

2. Mr. Lopez was the judge at the pie-baking contest.

3. Do you say the Pledge of Allegiance at your school?

4. Mrs. Chapman urged the students to get their projects done on time.

5. My little brother has truck designs on his pajamas.

6. Is that a genuine ruby in your ring?

7. Mitchell plays in the jazz band at school.

8. When Tom got in trouble, he lost his privileges at home.

9. What subjects do you think we should take next year?

10. In English class we have to write in our journal every day.

11. My mother has two pots of geraniums at the front door of our house.

12. Who was the strange man who visited the library?

13. There were six marriages on Saturday.

14. Let's all get together and make fudge this weekend.

15. Teresa said she didn't have any jewelry.

Consonant Sounds: *Exercise 20* WORD Pronunciation

WORD Pronunciation

Name: _____ Date: _____

Directions: Underline the words that have the consonant sound \k\ as in *keep, scold,* or *clock.* Use the dictionary if you need help. Circle the letters that spell the \k\ sound. Some sentences may have more than one word.

1. We took a scenic drive in the country.

2. Do you have any practical solutions to this problem?

3. Can you keep a secret, or do you tell everything?

4. I think your pants are too short; your ankles show.

5. Did you pack your lunch for the field trip?

6. What was Jay's favorite character in *Oliver Twist*?

7. Allison wants to be an architect when she grows up.

8. We put money in the jukebox to play music.

9. Mr. Chang put the key in the keyhole, but the lock wouldn't turn.

10. We are going to cancel the dance if more tickets aren't sold.

11. The spectators at the football game cheered for their team.

12. Everyone would like to win a scholarship to the computer camp.

13. The conductor on the train told us where our station was.

14. If you continue to consume more calories than you use, you will gain weight.

15. The brown caterpillar spun a cocoon and waited to become a butterfly.

Name: _____ Date: _____

Consonant Sounds: *Exercise 21* WORD Pronunciation

Directions: Underline the words that have the consonant sound \z\ as in *zoo* or *please*. Use the dictionary if you need help. Circle the letters that spell the \z\ sound. Some sentences may have more than one word.

1. Will you carry these plants to the greenhouse?

2. There was a zing in the sauce Mother made with hot peppers.

3. Please alphabetize the words before writing them on the paper.

4. Zoology is the science of animals.

5. Maize is the Indian name for corn.

6. The old movie comedies had zany characters in them.

7. When you have a cold, you sometimes wheeze when you breathe.

8. Suzanne used a zoom lens on her camera when she took the pictures.

9. This paper belongs with those on the desk.

10. The zipper broke on Phil's jacket when he tried to unzip it.

11. Do you realize that it takes millions of years to make a diamond?

12. In what time zone do you live?

13. Whose books were left on the table with mine?

14. The subzero temperatures in the Arctic make it difficult to live there.

15. These candy bars are yours and those candy bars are mine.

Consonant Sounds: *Exercise 22* WORD Pronunciation

Name: _____ Date: _____

Directions: Use your dictionary to write the pronunciation of each of the following words. Circle the letters that make consonant sounds \j\, soft \g\, \k\, hard \c\, soft \c\, and \z\.

1. fudge _____

2. keep _____

3. scold _____

4. just _____

5. these _____

6. ticket _____

7. smudge _____

8. zoology _____

9. soccer _____

10. please _____

11. chicken _____

12. zipper _____

13. those _____

14. judge _____

15. city _____

Name: _____ Date: _____

Consonant Sounds Review: *Crossword Puzzle* WORD Pronunciation

Directions: Write the correct spelling of each dictionary pronunciation below in the crossword puzzle.

ACROSS

3. sā′ lər
4. ə soom′
6. fē′ chər
7. ôk′ shən
11. prâr′ ē
12. wāv
14. ej′ oo kāt′ ər
16. test
18. kə koon′
19. kid′ nē

DOWN

1. brōk
2. fôlt
5. kwôr′ əl
6. frun′ tij
8. thûrd
9. dī′ pər
10. i maj′ in
13. dukt
15. ō′ mən
17. kon′ stənt

Name:_____ Date:_____

Consonant Sounds Review: *Word Search* WORD Pronunciation

Directions: Write the spelling of the word in the blank after the dictionary spelling. Then search for the word in the word search.

1. rān _____

2. stôrm _____

3. thun′ dər _____

4. wind _____

5. tôr nā′ dō _____

6. hāl _____

7. hûr′ i kān′ _____

8. līt′ ning _____

9. īs _____

10. snō _____

11. slēt _____

12. driz′ əl _____

```
F F X H F U W I U O M O I Q Z X C R L G
G V C E Q I I T A R K F C C B M W U Y X
D A A D L C U F B T J U S P Y Q I S G F
Y E N E V Z U R R O L F K I X T E N L T
A G X J I T Z D S R Q C B Y X F I I D I
J H I Q R C G I Q N W R A L R N X G P M
O R C W M F S N R A U I C P T D D U Z Z
P X V R A D E C I D S B N H W D M Y R J
A L O G C F N J M O T D G D Y H I E I I
T T A F B S Z T K F Y I I J W R D R G Z
S B R M O N M G E H L X M J K N R P V N
W R R Y H X U N X E T W N J U C G T P M
R H N O I U L B T R L X O H C R U U X A
R W D C J K R U Q N D S T G F S N O W C
C V M J P K W R Y X I M X S Y H N N X Q
L Y K L A V J V I E O A Q N B J Q H C O
H V Q L C U F D Z C T P R Y O E E Z Q T
W S K I G K U A R G A X S E V R K J A O
J F T A P J H T Y D D N G S W C S I Z T
Y L P H R O D K M E X T E Y I R S N I E
```

Vowel r Sounds: *Introduction*   WORD Pronunciation

There are three vowels with r sounds. When the two are put together, they make a new sound.

The sound \ôr\ is spelled "or." You hear the sound in words like *for* or *or.* It is sometimes spelled "ar" as in *quarter.*

The sound \ä\ is spelled "ar." You hear the sound in words like *car* or *part.* It is sometimes spelled "er" as in *sergeant.*

The sound \ûr\ is spelled several different ways. It is spelled "ir" in words such as *squirt.* It is also spelled "ur" in words such as *turn.* It is spelled "er" in words such as *butter.*

Name: _____ Date: _____

Vowel r Sounds: *Exercise 1*

WORD Pronunciation

Directions: Underline the words that have the vowel r sound \ûr\. Use the dictionary if you need help. Circle the letters that spell the \ûr\ sound. Some sentences may have more than one word.

1. Keith and his brother played in the dirt that had been delivered for the garden.

2. A whole flock of birds landed in our backyard.

3. The school nurse did the vision and hearing tests.

4. The art class used burlap to make their projects.

5. Blake's family is being transferred to Oregon.

6. Did you get a sunburn when you were at the swimming pool?

7. Conchita's favorite dessert is lime sherbet.

8. Where did Curt purchase his baseball cards?

9. Did you think the villain in the story was worthy of a pardon at the end?

10. Tom and Andre used mercury in their science experiment.

11. Our school sends out midterm reports to students who aren't doing well in class.

12. Mrs. Williams grows herbs on her kitchen windowsill.

13. The *Titanic* hit an iceberg and then sank.

14. You have to cite excerpts that you take from a book for your research paper.

15. Did you test the firmness of the ice before you stepped on it?

Name: _____ Date: _____

Vowel r Sounds: *Exercise 2* WORD Pronunciation

Directions: Underline the words that have the vowel r sound \ȯr\. Use the dictionary if you need help. Circle the letters that spell the \ȯr\ sound. Some sentences may have more than one word.

1. Paco grabbed an absorbent towel to soak up the spilled glass of water.

2. How will they transport the forty-five pianos to the other city?

3. Jennifer wants to work in a bookstore when she is old enough.

4. How many resources did Mrs. Cantrell say we needed for our paper?

5. Matt and Marty filled the cardboard boxes with things from their room.

6. We will have the assembly in the auditorium.

7. Pamela said she didn't have the coordination to be able to do gymnastics.

8. Corey forgot to read the story before class.

9. Blair's favorite food is corn on the cob.

10. Did Stacey hit her forehead when she went through the door?

11. My mom wants to be informed if we change our after-school plans.

12. We bought some boards to build the deck.

13. The violin performance was to be in the evening, but the performer was late.

14. Who is going to organize the committees for the school dance?

15. Did you start the tape recorder when the speech began?

60

Name: _____ Date: _____

Vowel r Sounds: *Exercise 3* WORD Pronunciation

Directions: Underline the words that have the vowel r sound \ä\. Use the dictionary if you need help. Circle the letters that spell the \ä\ sound. Some sentences may have more than one word.

1. How far is it from California to New York?

2. There are superstars in sports and in entertainment.

3. The Arctic Ocean is near the North Pole.

4. When my grandmother was a little girl, she rode the streetcar to go to the city.

5. Belinda learned archery when she was at camp during the summer.

6. The crystal sparkled after it was washed and dried.

7. Mrs. Greeger said it takes hard work to become an artist.

8. Sandra and Marta made rhubarb pies to sell at the bake sale.

9. Carson still felt sleepy when his alarm rang this morning.

10. When we square dance, we swing our partner and go round and round.

11. If you use cardboard on the back, your poster will stand up straighter.

12. The marsh had beautiful ferns and little flowers.

13. For our trip to London, we can only take a garment bag and a small suitcase.

14. The Texas barbecue was a big noisy party.

15. Mr. Kaye was a sergeant in the army for twenty years.

Vowel r Sounds: *Exercise 4*

WORD Pronunciation

Name: _____   Date: _____

Directions: Use your dictionary to write the pronunciation of each of the following words. Circle the letters that make the vowel r sound.

1. worn-out   _____

2. reserve   _____

3. assorted   _____

4. cafeteria   _____

5. occur   _____

6. watermelon   _____

7. dander   _____

8. burlap   _____

9. security   _____

10. research   _____

11. leader   _____

12. orthodontist   _____

13. underwater   _____

14. sherbet   _____

15. heart   _____

Vowel r Sounds: *Exercise 5*

Name: _____ Date: _____

WORD Pronunciation

Directions: Look at the dictionary pronunciation of the word. Circle the vowel r sound on the dictionary spelling in red. Write the usual spelling of the word on the blank. Circle the vowel r sound on the usual spelling in red. Use the word in a sentence.

1. här′ dn   _____

    _____

2. bôr′ dər   _____

    _____

3. bûrth′ dā′   _____

    _____

4. skwûrt   _____

    _____

5. gûrl   _____

    _____

6. pärt′ nər   _____

    _____

7. stôr′ ē   _____

    _____

8. gär′ dn   _____

    _____

63

Vowel r Sounds: *Exercise 6*

WORD Pronunciation

Directions: Look at the dictionary pronunciation of the word. Circle the vowel r sound on the dictionary spelling in red. Write the usual spelling of the word on the blank. Circle the vowel r sound on the usual spelling in red. Use the word in a sentence.

1. cär′ nə vəl _____

   _____

2. pärt _____

   _____

3. pûr′ chəs _____

   _____

4. pər haps′ _____

   _____

5. bär′ tər _____

   _____

6. skâr _____

   _____

7. tŏŏr′ nə mənt _____

   _____

8. ôr′ nə mənt _____

   _____

Schwa Sound: *Introduction* WORD Pronunciation

The schwa is the sound \uh\. It is an unclear sound that most often occurs in the unaccented syllable of words, but sometimes it is also shown in accented syllables. It is represented by the upside-down\ə\. The schwa can represent any of the vowels.

val′ ən tīn′	valentine
pər mit′	permit
bə nan′ ə	banana
bit′ ər	bitter
tə māt′ o	tomato
ē′ *th*ər	either

The schwa is the most common vowel sound in the English language.

Name: _____ Date: _____

Schwa Sound: *Exercise 1*

WORD Pronunciation

Directions: Use your dictionary to write the pronunciation of each of the following words. Circle the letter that makes the schwa sound in the dictionary pronunciation. Some words may not have a schwa sound.

1. diet _____

2. apricot _____

3. seldom _____

4. minute _____

5. opera _____

6. family _____

7. minus _____

8. polish _____

9. practical _____

10. debonair _____

11. correspondence _____

12. propel _____

13. originate _____

14. blizzard _____

15. apron _____

Name:_____ Date:_____

Schwa Sound: *Exercise 2*

WORD Pronunciation

Directions: Underline the words that have the schwa sound \ə\. Use the dictionary if you need help. Circle the letters that spell the \ə\ sound. Some sentences may have more than one word. On the line below each sentence, write the dictionary spellings of the schwa words.

1. I need to get my paper from my desk.

    _____

2. Who asked the teacher the last question?

    _____

3. Four plus seven equals eleven.

    _____

4. The house was very quiet when I got home.

    _____

5. Did you go to the festival?

    _____

6. I purchased a medium sweatshirt.

    _____

7. The instructor said that Jan danced well.

    _____

8. The chemicals we use in science class are in the bottles.

    _____

Name:_____ Date: _____

Schwa Sound: *Exercise 3*

WORD Pronunciation

Directions: Underline the words that have the schwa sound \ə\. Use the dictionary if you need help. Circle the letters that spell the \ə\ sound. Some sentences may have more than one word. On the line below each sentence, write the dictionary spellings of the schwa words.

1. The infant was crying loudly.

    _____

2. Will you please polish the table?

    _____

3. For what occasions do you give gifts?

    _____

4. My mom wears an apron when she cooks.

    _____

5. Tim fixed lemonade to drink.

    _____

6. Last winter our town had a blizzard.

    _____

7. Maggie is going to paint and stencil her room.

    _____

8. I had a pickle on my hamburger.

    _____

Other Sounds: *Introduction*

\ȯ\ - is a vowel sound. You hear it in words like *tall* and *flaw.*

\oi\ - is a vowel sound. You hear it in words like *toil* and *toy.*

\o͝o\ - is a short vowel sound. You hear it in words like *hook* and *look.*

\o͞o\ - is a long vowel sound. You hear it in words like *zoo* and *tool.*

\ou\ - is a vowel sound. You hear it in words like *how* and *our.*

\ch\ - is a consonant sound. You hear it in words like *church* and *teach.*

\hw\ - is a consonant sound. You hear it in words like *where* and *which.*

\ng\ - is a consonant sound. You hear it in words like *ring* and *marching.*

\sh\ - is a consonant sound. You hear it in words like *shelf* and *mush.*

\th\ - is a consonant sound. You hear it in words like *think* and *myth.*

th\ - is a consonant sound. You hear it in words like *the* and *this.*

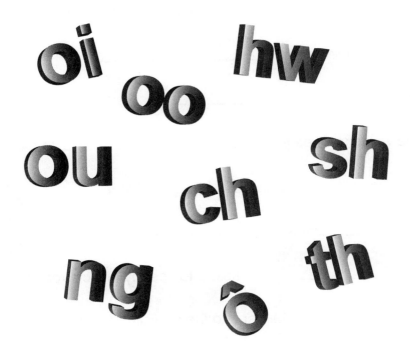

69

Name: _____ Date: _____

Other Sounds: *Exercise 1*   WORD Pronunciation

Directions: Complete the following sentences with words that have the sound \ȯ\. Use the dictionary if you need help.

rainfall	lawyer	nightfall	hotel	alternate	hauled
chopper	fault	cloth	chocolate	oblong	watermelon
flaw	salty	draw	officer	sometimes	chalkboard

1. There was a _____ in the china saucer.

2. Mrs. Wang told three people to work out their problems on the _____.

3. How much _____ is in the rain gauge?

4. Jake and I had to take an _____ route to school yesterday.

5. The police officer said the accident wasn't the man's _____.

6. Ben wants to be a _____ when he grows up.

7. For our math homework, Kevin drew three _____ figures.

8. By _____ the campers had set up their camp.

9. A favorite summertime treat is _____.

10. The pretzels tasted _____ .

11. The costume will take three yards of _____ to make.

12. In art class Felipe will _____ still-lifes.

13. _____ cake is my favorite dessert.

14. The police _____ asked to see my bicycle registration.

15. We _____ the cans to the recycling station.

70

Name: _____   Date: _____

Other Sounds: *Exercise 2*   WORD Pronunciation

Directions: Complete the following sentences with words that have the sound \oi\. Use the dictionary if you need help.

pointer	cope	hard-boiled	joints	boyhood	money
decoys	oil	adjoining	subsoil	toys	toil
joy	noise	ploy	destroyed	hoot	employed

1. Mark Twain's _____ home was in Hannibal, Missouri.

2. The archaeologists dug down to the _____ looking for artifacts.

3. Matt's little brother _____ his scale model bridge.

4. Jessica and Anna packed _____ eggs and sandwiches for their picnic.

5. My sister hopes to be _____ this summer to make money for college.

6. My grandmother says that her _____ hurt her in the morning.

7. Helen is going to _____ her bicycle after school today.

8. When families get together, there is much _____.

9. Mr. Rodriguez and Mrs. Evans have _____ classrooms.

10. The twins received many _____ for their birthday.

11. Lauren used the _____ to show us where France was on the map.

12. The _____ outside our classroom was distracting during the test.

13. The football team used a fake field goal as a _____ to win the game.

14. It is hard work to _____ in the fields during the summer.

15. The hunter put _____ on the lake to attract the ducks.

Name: _____ Date: _____

Other Sounds: *Exercise 3*   WORD Pronunciation

Directions: Complete the following sentences with words that have the sound \ŏŏ\. Use the dictionary if you need help.

books	loom	hood	wool	stood	woodpecker
tour	door	nook	good	hoof	took
brook	cook	tooth	poor	shook	looking

1. Would you please carry the _____ to the library?

2. Jesse and Michael are going to go on a bicycle _____ of their town.

3. The slides were unclear; they were of _____ quality.

4. Jessica had a furry _____ on her parka.

5. Who _____ the red pencil from the box?

6. The path led across the _____ and down into the forest.

7. The noisy _____ was pecking at our roof this morning.

8. Which _____ on the horse needs a new shoe?

9. The sheep had stiff, ivory-colored _____.

10. Our class had to check every _____ and cranny for the missing hamster.

11. The dog _____ at the back door waiting to come into the house.

12. What book are you _____ for in the library?

13. Emily _____ the bottle of paint to mix the colors.

14. Caroline thought it was her turn to _____ dinner tonight.

15. Nick and Cameron were _____ hockey players.

72

Name: _____ Date: _____

Other Sounds: *Exercise 4* WORD Pronunciation

Directions: Complete the following sentences with words that have the sound \o͞o\. Use the dictionary if you need help.

cool	noon	too	school	mood	oozed
moor	hoop	fool	door	shoot	brood
gloomy	food	boots	cook	spoons	root

1. The toothpaste _____ from the tube.

2. The twins try to _____ people when they change places.

3. Luis wanted to go on the field trip _____.

4. The sailor was to _____ the boat to the dock when they landed.

5. Brenda and Bethany were sure there was enough _____ for the party.

6. Alonzo turned the fan so the _____ air would reach the whole room.

7. The mother hen watched over her _____ of baby chicks.

8. Don't forget to wear your _____ out in the snow.

9. The basketball went through the _____ for two points.

10. Are potatoes and carrots _____ vegetables?

11. I wish we ate lunch at _____ instead of earlier.

12. Liz set the table with the _____ on the left side of the plate.

13. Karal, Jon, and Megan are going to _____ baskets after school today.

14. Which _____ will you be going to next year?

15. Henry was in a good _____ after he saw his science grade.

Name: _____   Date: _____

Other Sounds: *Exercise 5*   WORD Pronunciation

Directions: Complete the following sentences with words that have the sound \ou\. Use the dictionary if you need help.

downhill	cloves	outdoors	sound	announce	amount
foul	chop	rebound	eyebrows	chow	crowd
clouds	house	fountain	drowning	home	drought

1. I couldn't go _____; the snow was too deep.

2. During the tornado drill, no one was to make a _____.

3. The basketball player caught the _____ and shot the winning basket.

4. Susan realized she had used the wrong _____ of flour in the cookie recipe.

5. Benita and Will told Denise to meet them at their _____.

6. Caitlin drew dark _____ on her mask for the play.

7. Laurie likes to look at the _____ and see what shapes they resemble.

8. The marathon racecourse was planned to go uphill and _____.

9. We have to line up to use the drinking _____.

10. Marilyn was to _____ the winners of the art contest.

11. The country had so little rain that it was having a _____.

12. The hockey player committed a _____ and had to sit out for two minutes.

13. Mai and Cody stood in the huge _____ waiting for the parade.

14. Candice took swimming lessons to help protect her from _____.

15. A slang word for food is _____.

Name:_____   Date: _____

Other Sounds: *Exercise 6*   WORD Pronunciation

Directions: Use your dictionary to write the pronunciation of each of the following words.

1. look   _____

2. toil   _____

3. zoo   _____

4. drown   _____

5. windfall   _____

6. joyful   _____

7. bookcase   _____

8. foolproof   _____

9. flaw   _____

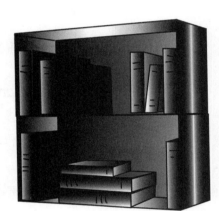

10. drought   _____

11. our   _____

12. hard-boiled   _____

13. enjoy   _____

14. caught   _____

15. downhill   _____

Name:_____ Date:_____

Other Sounds: *Exercise 7* ## WORD Pronunciation

Directions: Underline the words that have the sound \ch\ as in *teach* and *church*. Use the dictionary if you need help. Circle the letters that spell the \ch\ sound. Some sentences may have more than one word.

1. The television station dispatched a news team to the fire.

2. Be careful that you don't choke on the cherry pit.

3. Linda had to crouch down to get under the table to get the pen.

4. The church on the corner planted a tree in the yard.

5. Mrs. McDowell has a chart on the wall that tells us how many books we have read.

6. We have to choose our favorite character from the book and write about him or her.

7. Did you change your schedule so that you will have gym in the morning?

8. My mom made a batch of chocolate chip cookies.

9. We check our math homework every day.

10. The dog snatched the bone and ran around the yard with it.

11. The check for five dollars was attached to the permission slip.

12. Jackson tried to match the question cards with the answer cards.

13. Did Lewis or Frank reach the top of the hill first?

14. Amber baked a peach pie for dessert.

15. Has a president ever been impeached?

Name: _____ Date: _____

Other Sounds: *Exercise 8*   **WORD Pronunciation**

Directions: Underline the words that have the sound \hw\ as in *where* or *when*. Use the dictionary if you need help. Circle the letters that spell the \hw\ sound. Some sentences may have more than one word.

1. Where did you put your homework?

2. I don't know whether to eat lunch at school or to go home.

3. Ryan asked, "Did you see my pens anywhere?"

4. Cassie would like to know when this paper is due.

5. Which actor is playing the lead in the play?

6. The horses whinnied softly when we entered the barn.

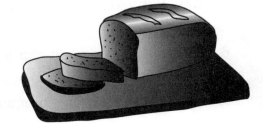

7. Did you see the huge tankers coming into the wharf?

8. Will the wheat bread have more nutrition than the white bread?

9. What whaling town is on the eastern shore?

10. Why did Ashley leave school so early?

11. Some people with a cold wheeze when they breathe.

12. Which nursery rhyme includes the word *whey*?

13. Wang gave his little sister a ride in the wheelbarrow.

14. You could hear the whack of the bat as it hit the ball in the game.

15. Wherever you go on your vacation, write about it in your journal.

Name: _____ Date: _____

Other Sounds: *Exercise 9*

WORD Pronunciation

Directions: Underline the words that have the sound \ng\ as in *ring* and *marching.* Use the dictionary if you need help. Circle the letters that spell the \ng\ sound. Some sentences may have more than one word.

1. Are Miguel and Patrick singing in the school choir this year?

2. My class is planning a trip to Washington, D.C., next year.

3. Were you studying last night for the test?

4. Mom told me to use the tongs rather than my hands to pick up the ice.

5. Mrs. Barry told us not to use slang in our formal writing.

6. Are you whistling part of the song you heard on the radio?

7. A fork has four or five prongs called tines.

8. Natalie and Paul received a detention for whispering during reading time.

9. The guitar string went twang before it broke.

10. Janet wanted to take a foreign language next year in school.

11. Do you think Mrs. Bradshaw will lead the debating team next year?

12. We threw pennies in the old wishing well.

13. Do you know someone who lives in Lansing, Michigan?

14. Pedro has been working on his Boy Scout project since last spring.

15. Are we going to be melting wax to make the candles?

Other Sounds: *Exercise 10*

WORD Pronunciation

Directions: Underline the words that have the sound \sh\ as in *shelf* and *mush.* Use the dictionary if you need help. Circle the letters that spell the \sh\ sound. Some sentences may have more than one word.

1. She asked her teacher how to do the science experiment.

2. Megan is very good at drawing fashion models.

3. Some doors you need to push, and some doors you need to pull.

4. Make sure you shake the trash bag open before you try to fill it.

5. The last thing my mother told me as I left the house was to brush my hair.

6. Do you think wishing wells ever really make wishes come true?

7. The shabby chair ended up in the basement.

8. The kindergarten students were learning to tie their shoes.

9. The shading and the shadows made the drawing look very lifelike.

10. The curtains were too sheer to keep out the sunlight.

11. My dad and I planted several shrubs in our front yard.

12. My brother and I built a shack to use as our clubhouse.

13. Please shut the window before you go to the magic show.

14. The girls shrieked as they won their shuffleboard game.

15. Did you push the shreds of cloth onto the floor?

Name:_____ Date: _____

Other Sounds: *Exercise 11*

WORD Pronunciation

Directions: Underline the words that have the sound \th\ as in *think* and *myth*. Use the dictionary if you need help. Circle the letters that spell the \th\ sound. Some sentences may have more than one word.

1. The thin line on the floor divided the two teams.

2. What path are we to take to get to the cabin?

3. I pinched my thumb in the screen door.

4. The dark clouds threatened rain and we thought they would cancel the baseball game.

5. James asked to have the ball thrown to him.

6. Ether was used during the Civil War to help the injured during surgery.

7. There were myths written about Greeks and Romans.

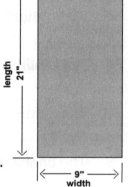

8. It is important to take care of your health all your life.

9. To get the area of the rectangle, you multiply the length times the width.

10. The old carpet was worn and threadbare.

11. In what month of the year were you born?

12. The throttle on the steam engine was difficult to move.

13. Did you walk through the front door or through the back door?

14. When someone is mad, you sometimes feel their wrath.

15. The queen and the king both sit on a throne.

Name: _____   Date: _____

Other Sounds: *Exercise 12*   WORD Pronunciation

Directions: Underline the words that have the sound \th\ as in *the* or *this*. Use the dictionary if you need help. Circle the letters that spell the \th\ sound. Some sentences may have more than one word.

1. That coat and hat belong to Beverly.

2. I wish we could either read or go to the library today.

3. Rosa bathed her little sister before putting her to bed.

4. Steven wondered if the pencil was his or if it belonged to Josh.

5. The new car made the rough road seem smooth.

6. My brother is going to college next year.

7. The robin's feathers floated slowly to the ground.

8. Are your mother and father coming to the school open house?

9. Mr. Stephens said that the work of the committee was praiseworthy.

10. Ling thought even though the science experiment failed, he had learned some things.

11. I think we need to work on our project tonight; otherwise it will be turned in late.

12. These shoes are too tight for my feet.

13. I think they need a ride home from the playground.

14. Some people tithe money to their church.

15. Matthew would rather go to the movie than the baseball game.

81

Name:_____ Date:_____

Other Sounds: *Exercise 13*

WORD Pronunciation

Directions: Use your dictionary to write the pronunciation of each of the following words.

1. this _____

2. which _____

3. catch _____

4. pathway _____

5. father _____

6. whose _____

7. that _____

8. brush _____

9. shriek _____

10. wash _____

11. bringing _____

12. teacher _____

13. song _____

14. mother _____

15. bathe _____

Accent Marks: *Introduction* WORD Pronunciation

Accent marks are used to show which syllable is pronounced with greater stress than the others. The dictionary only marks words that have two or more syllables with accent marks.

In a dictionary the word will be divided into syllables. There will be a light accent mark on the syllable with the secondary accent and a dark accent mark on the syllable with the primary accent.

It is important to pay attention to accent marks. If you stress the wrong syllable, it will change the pronunciation of the word and sometimes the meaning.

stairway	ster′ wā
lazy	lā′ zē
address	ad′ res
address	ə dres′

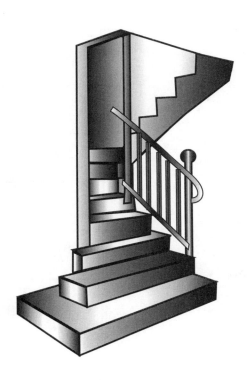

83

Name:_____ Date:_____

Accent Marks: *Exercise 1*

WORD Pronunciation

Directions: Write these words in syllables. Then look them up in your dictionary to see which syllable or syllables are accented. Mark the accents in red.

1. ankle _____

2. coppersmith _____

3. semicolon _____

4. deserved _____

5. terrain _____

6. grandstand _____

7. manager _____

8. projection _____

9. outspoken _____

10. propel _____

11. marriage _____

12. investigation _____

13. microphone _____

14. cafeteria _____

15. farmyard _____

Name: _____ Date: _____

Accent Marks: *Exercise 2*

WORD Pronunciation

Directions: Write these words in syllables. Then look them up in your dictionary to see which syllable or syllables are accented. Mark the accents in red.

1. prevent _____

2. radar _____

3. decide _____

4. leopard _____

5. opponent _____

6. audition _____

7. tropical _____

8. thrust _____

9. impact _____

10. engaged _____

11. defensive _____

12. textile _____

13. crossbar _____

14. mountain _____

15. crucial _____

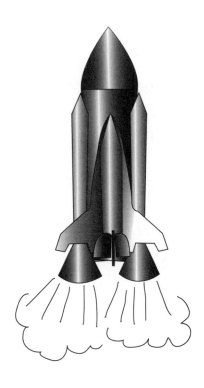

Name:_____ Date:_____

Accent Marks: *Exercise 3*

WORD Pronunciation

Directions: The following words can be pronounced two different ways. Look in the dictionary for the two pronunciations and write them on the lines.

1. either _____   _____

2. defense _____   _____

3. tomato _____   _____

4. caramel _____   _____

5. rodeo _____   _____

6. perfect _____   _____

7. minute _____   _____

8. record _____   _____

9. rebel _____   _____

10. refuse _____   _____

Which words are just pronounced differently and which words have different meanings when pronounced differently? Choose two of the words that have different meanings when pronounced differently. Write a sentence for each meaning. (That is a total of four sentences.)

_____

_____

_____

_____

Word Pronunciation Review: *Crossword Puzzle*

Name: _____ Date: _____

Directions: Write the correct spelling of each dictionary pronunciation below in the crossword puzzle.

ACROSS

3. tō′ stər
4. sun′ flou′ ər
8. mā′ pəl
9. al′ ə gā′ tər
13. fash′ ən
14. en′ ē hou′
17. lē′ dər
18. sēs′ lis

DOWN

1. trō′ fē
2. swift′ lē
3. trans lāt′
5. jaz
6. jent′ lē
7. yūth
10. in′ ə sənt
11. dub′ əl
12. ri sīt′
13. fung′ gəs
15. nik′ əl
16. kēp

Name: _____ Date: _____

Word Pronunciation Review: *Word Search* WORD Pronunciation

Directions: Write the word from each dictionary pronunciation on the line following it. Then search for the word in the word search.

1. ter′ ə fī′ _____
2. ō′ vər wûrk′ _____
3. rē′ fund′ _____
4. prīd _____
5. mith _____
6. ī dē′ ə _____
7. dol′ ər _____
8. fēt _____
9. bas′ kit _____
10. hāst _____
11. kən fes′ _____
12. mīn _____

```
R O W P B H Q X D I H T Y M S C G P N Q
W Y V G O O A A U X R H N T E V V B L K
X S H E V M B E J A P H T N E X F N W X
H O M Q R G T X P Y H A C W N K B B G C
T Z V H E W E V A R A M Z A H V S P X S
R A S D V D O S I F E E T N Y Z B A N I
B F G O X O B R T N K X B W I O N Y B H
K F J Z A E D I K D S I K M D W F Y O P
F P W U B L I H B F S A G F D U R H L B
D A L V A W C C U U V Z M R W N B D K X
R Y Y V J O F L J B B E X K A Z U X K H
S F B D N F D V V S B D E R V X F F U Z
X V Q F P Q X Q K S H I B K N R I I E S
S V E S I S Q E H Q R R U B V U Q O R R
N S N A D V V A I M N P A Z E W V J I X
S T R C V A S Y A M I P Q I N A J J U R
N M R R Y T P J S V L A C V I E N I M V
F K S Q E M J F R A L L O D U N C W J O
E L L U I U C W D M K R R R J A G G C V
H R L U S Y F I R R E T T Q G R J N T B
```

88

Answer Keys

Letters that students are to circle will be in boldface and underlined. Teacher check circled letters on original words.

Short Vowels: Exercise 1 (p. 3)
1. admit
2. flash
3. matador
4. saddle
5. appetite
6. active
7. disaster
8. cafeteria
9. ask
10. example
11. facts
12. Perhaps
13. sad
14. subtract
15. salad

Short Vowels: Exercise 2 (p. 4)
1. accelerate
2. midafternoon
3. capture
4. vanity
5. fashion
6. laminate
7. valentine
8. sandal

Short Vowels: Exercise 3 (p. 5)
1. met
2. bench
3. closet
4. definitions
5. neck
6. less
7. open
8. letter
9. check
10. hundred
11. left
12. established
13. forget
14. tennis
15. sentences

Short Vowels: Exercise 4 (p. 6)
1. reservoir
2. attachment
3. selfish
4. propellent
5. genuine
6. fennel
7. energize
8. fiesta

Short Vowels: Exercise 5 (p. 7)
1. switch
2. different
3. drilled
4. active
5. drift
6. picture
7. beautiful
8. live
9. fish
10. gigantic
11. punishment
12. slippery
13. trip
14. admit
15. fit

Short Vowels: Exercise 6 (p. 8)
1. figure
2. athletic
3. disable
4. critical
5. rheumatism
6. mischief
7. bridging
8. nickel

Short Vowels: Exercise 7 (p. 9)
1. dog's
2. common
3. robber
4. plot
5. jukebox
6. improper
7. Geology
8. crocodile
9. soccer
10. pond
11. binoculars
12. anybody
13. compactor
14. monogrammed
15. chopped

Short Vowels: Exercise 8 (p. 10)
1. operator
2. fondness
3. chopsticks
4. cottage
5. body
6. spotless
7. botany
8. compact

Short Vowels: Exercise 9 (p. 11)
1. brush
2. sculptor
3. supper
4. hunter
5. blushed
6. fluttered
7. sunrise
8. cucumber
9. pulse
10. puppet
11. summer
12. run
13. crunches
14. industries
15. chuckled

Short Vowels: Exercise 10 (p. 12)
1. cultivate
2. button
3. engulf
4. guzzle
5. industrious
6. blunt
7. injustice
8. tunnel

Short Vowels: Exercise 11 (p. 13)
1. long, have, lived, in, Quincy, Illinois
2. asked, picnic, with, them
3. is, going, with, dad
4. have
5. and, asked, Allison, with, them
6. Is, milk, thing, drink, at, lunch-time
7. is, that
8. think, six, pencils, in, box, when, opened, it
9. Tim, will, bring, Matt, and, Kim, celebration
10. dog, have
11. Can, soccer
12. think, have, dishes, after, dinner
13. is, helping, us
14. This, is, difficult, assignment
15. window, when

Short Vowels: Exercise 12 (p. 14)
1. en thōō′ zē as′ tik
2. peng′ gwin
3. ə pren′ tis ship′
4. kaf′ ə tir′ ē ə
5. trus tē′
6. swift′ lē
7. kan′ yən
8. brush
9. kon′ fər əns
10. im plant′
11. gran′ it
12. rap
13. un′ fôr′ chə nit
14. twen′ tē
15. shə lak′

Short Vowels: Exercise 13 (p. 15)
1. plā′ pen′
2. kap′ chər
3. di bāt′
4. fol′ ō
5. bə lis′ tik
6. les′ ôr′
7. wond
8. felt
9. ə ston′ ish d
10. ling′ gō
11. pok′ it
12. vast
13. yel′ ō
14. nim′ bəl
15. i rek′ tər

Long Vowels: Exercise 1 (p. 17)
1. play
2. incorporate
3. highway
4. praise
5. vacancies
6. bake
7. cable
8. weighs
9. stadium
10. betray
11. tame
12. eighth
13. frail
14. layer
15. details

Long Vowels: Exercise 2 (p. 18)
1. alternate
2. coordination
3. favor
4. daze
5. postnatal
6. failing
7. occasion
8. recreation

89

Long Vowels: Exercise 3 (p. 19)
1. retrieve
2. leotards
3. medium
4. field
5. obvious
6. peacocks
7. chimney
8. eager
9. seized
10. decompose
11. referee
12. scream
13. receive
14. vehicles
15. believe

Long Vowels: Exercise 4 (p. 20)
1. ordinaril**y**
2. b**e**li**e**f
3. archer**y**
4. b**ea**st
5. ster**e**ophonic
6. scr**ea**m
7. rec**ei**ve
8. k**e**yhole

Long Vowels: Exercise 5 (p. 21)
1. I, need, medium, sized
2. eat
3. I, Jane, race
4. cake, ice, cream
5. Tyler, going, play, year
6. I, homework, tomorrow
7. Blake, say, they, going, over
8. playing, right
9. I, we, snow
10. three, rain
11. five, eight
12. grows
13. Amy, needs, science
14. green, blue, paper
15. day, assignment

Long Vowels: Exercise 6 (p. 22)
1. pine
2. pride
3. wind
4. unify
5. five
6. cider
7. high
8. strike
9. identical
10. might
11. sky
12. license
13. final
14. reply
15. ice

Long Vowels: Exercise 7 (p. 23)
1. p**i**pe
2. t**i**tle
3. reli**a**ble
4. g**y**rate
5. unif**y**
6. civil**i**ze
7. b**i**monthly
8. cl**i**mb

Long Vowels: Exercise 8 (p. 24)
1. float
2. trombone
3. slopes
4. both
5. note
6. antisocial
7. zoology
8. show
9. notice
10. follow
11. oath
12. toast
13. swallowed
14. widow
15. vote

Long Vowels: Exercise 9 (p. 25)
1. transp**o**se
2. swall**ow**
3. turb**o**jet
4. dec**o**de
5. disp**o**se
6. dr**o**ne
7. audi**o**visual
8. bif**o**cal

Long Vowels: Exercise 10 (p. 26)
1. fuel
2. gratitude
3. dispute
4. cucumbers
5. university
6. unicycles
7. mutual
8. humid
9. discontinued
10. solitude
11. united
12. continued
13. utensil
14. tube
15. dude

Long Vowels: Exercise 11 (p. 27)
1. t**u**be
2. **u**tensil
3. gen**ui**ne
4. m**u**tual
5. n**ui**sance
6. st**u**dio
7. **u**nify
8. barbec**ue**

Long Vowels: Exercise 12 (p. 28)
1. sub′ z**ē**′ r**ō**
2. s**ō**′ shəl
3. ə p**ē**l′
4. st**ū**′ d**ē ō**′
5. grat′ ə f**ī**′
6. im′ pə l**ī**t′
7. d**ā**z
8. **ē**′ ger nes
9. p**ē**′ k**ō**k′
10. p**ī**nt
11. n**ī**n′ t**ē**n′
12. k**ē**′ h**ō**l′
13. p**ā**n′ tər
14. l**ē**′ ə tärd′
15. str**ē**t′ kär′

Long Vowels: Exercise 13 (p. 29)
1. kə n**ī**v′
2. t**ū**′ nik
3. m**ō**ld
4. g**ā**n′ ər
5. b**ā**′ ber′ **ē**
6. sk**ī**
7. fr**ē**k
8. b**ī** ol′ ə j**ē**
9. trans p**ō**z′
10. m**ā**d′ n
11. d**ē**′ pən
12. s**oo**′ pər v**ī**z′
13. **ō**′ vər fl**ō**′
14. p**ō**st d**ā**t′
15. en l**ī**t′ n

Short and Long Vowels Review: Crossword (p. 30)

Short and Long Vowels Review: Word Search (p. 31)
1. gain
2. knot
3. remove
4. tempt
5. juggle
6. denim
7. ocean
8. phoney
9. hockey
10. gelatin
11. bitter
12. depress

Word Search:

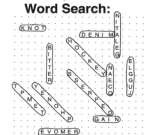

Consonant Sounds: Exercise 1 (p. 33)
1. **b**irch, **b**ackyard
2. **b**rought, ham**b**urger, **b**uns, **b**arbecue
3. **b**rother, **b**oth, tu**b**a, **b**and
4. **b**rown, **b**anana
5. ra**bb**it, warm-**b**looded
6. su**b**way
7. a**b**sent
8. su**b**zero
9. **B**eth, **b**lushed, **B**est
10. **b**anquet
11. **b**ushes, **b**ags
12. **b**ilingual, **b**oth
13. **B**en, **b**ites, **b**ody
14. ro**b**in
15. **b**us

Consonant Sounds: Exercise 2 (p. 34)
1. **d**og, un**d**erneath
2. **d**irections, sai**d**, **d**escribe
3. a**dd**ress
4. **d**own
5. to**d**ay, **d**reary
6. gra**d**es, mi**d**-year
7. **d**ust
8. **d**oes
9. **d**ime, **d**ull
10. Woul**d**, la**dd**er, to**d**ay
11. wi**d**ow, husban**d**, **d**ied
12. Chil**d**ren's, un**d**er, toa**d**stools
13. nee**d**ed, tripo**d**
14. stoppe**d**, roa**d**side
15. **d**ifficult, **d**eal, ru**d**e

Consonant Sounds: Exercise 3 (p. 35)
1. **f**ly
2. **f**eathers, **f**loated, **f**rom
3. **f**ungus
4. Je**ff**, **f**arewell,

friends
5. father, fall
6. fell, fractured
7. puff
8. fresh, firmness
9. fiesta
10. fluffy, fuzz
11. fountain, Frances
12. formula, for
13. forehead, frame
14. faculty, family
15. forty, fifty, leaf, for, fair

Consonant Sounds: Exercise 4 (p. 36)
1. got, gardenia
2. granite
3. guardian
4. glisten
5. Garcia, gossip
6. garden, grow
7. ground, gate
8. Ghana
9. grip, gross, frog
10. green, gray
11. grandpa, gramophone
12. Grant
13. grammar
14. Gregory, gutters
15. ghosts

Consonant Sounds: Exercise 5 (p. 37)
1. hero
2. have, hawk
3. Hard-boiled, halves
4. hats, hooks, be-hind
5. hens, hiding
6. Harris, high
7. had, hedgehog
8. hauled
9. hurry, hot
10. haze
11. Haley, headfirst
12. heart, healthy
13. history, heritage
14. hired, horses

15. homonyms, home

Consonant Sounds: Exercise 6 (p. 38)
1. follow, lawyer
2. candles, lantern, lights
3. locked
4. lazy, ladder
5. lavender, yellow
6. lacked, color, pencil
7. lunar, looked, like
8. lemonade, lukewarm
9. landscape, leaves
10. lunch, earlier
11. let, lesson, slip
12. Alex, leverage, large
13. less, population, Latvia, Lithuania
14. list
15. litter, little

Consonant Sounds: Exercise 7 (p. 39)
1. members, family
2. midweek
3. mystery
4. summer, family, Munich, Germany
5. musicians, musicals
6. Mrs., Smith, modified, math, assignment
7. Monica, mutual, Minneapolis, Minnesota
8. minimum, amount
9. Jamie, mimick-ing, animals
10. mercury, thermometers, Miriam
11. Madam, monsieur
12. magician, came,

magic
13. mountain, America
14. magazines
15. my, monogram

Consonant Sounds: Exercise 8 (p. 40)
1. numerous
2. Kevin, never, answered, question
3. noticeable, front
4. Enrique, nickels, nine
5. Student, Council, needs, find, on
6. Sean's, nuisance
7. Ben, needs, nightfall
8. Cardinals', no-hitter, in
9. miners, nuggets
10. Linda's, nineteen
11. name, nameless
12. dinner, noodles, chicken
13. narrow, ribbon
14. Many, nation, presidents
15. notify, Grayson, running

Consonant Sounds: Exercise 9 (p. 41)
1. Pledge
2. Panama, peacock, patio
3. papa, patches, pants
4. proof, pen
5. mop
6. presentation, perfect
7. project, puppet
8. pumpkin, pie, pudding
9. pack, trip, Pennsylvania
10. sparrow, perched, pole

11. pop, popcorn
12. postscript
13. pints, pint
14. preserve, pickles
15. panel, posters

Consonant Sounds: Exercise 10 (p. 42)
1. James, sandals, sandy
2. squirrel, scampered, across, sidewalk
3. must, self-confident, stand, school, speech
4. smog, San Francisco
5. science, smell, classroom
6. selfish, toys
7. Samantha, spike
8. squad, raise, school, spirit
9. stamp
10. say, stapler, staple
11. exercise, substantial
12. wears, such, stylish, clothes
13. strange, things, just, swallow
14. Baseball, players, sunflower, seeds
15. suit

Consonant Sounds: Exercise 11 (p. 43)
1. little, toothless, turtle, street
2. getting, grants, to, technology
3. tomatoes, rotten
4. transplanted, tree, front, to
5. trophy, tournament
6. treasurer
7. tending
8. time

9. took, tulips, arrangement
10. toast, breakfast
11. thought, meat, too, tough, to, cut
12. not, let, get, tattoo
13. tear, tablecloth
14. tornado, effect, until, midnight
15. tortillas, to, tacos

Consonant Sounds: Exercise 12 (p. 44)
1. vary
2. vacancy
3. various, vitamins
4. vane
5. variety
6. visited, violinist
7. vehicles
8. vanilla
9. veterans, having, November
10. vicious
11. have, vinegar
12. veto
13. voyages
14. velvet
15. venture, very

Consonant Sounds: Exercise 13 (p. 45)
1. watermelons
2. wallet, walking
3. watch, weeknights
4. would, warm, sweater
5. walnut
6. wants, weather
7. wear, winter
8. always, sand-wich
9. wind, windsock, was
10. wand, wishes
11. Would, woodcarver
12. westward, wagons

91

13. **w**iggle
14. **w**ere, **w**obbly
15. **w**alked, **w**eb, **w**ay

Consonant Sounds: Exercise 14 (p. 46)
1. pri tend′
2. ō′ vər bôrd′
3. mi stāk′
4. ad mīr′
5. wēk′ nĭt′
6. di pär′ chər
7. kas′ əl
8. wig′ əl
9. ul′ tə mit
10. kwôr′ tər
11. sē′ nik
12. pûr′ pəs
13. səg jest′
14. kom′ pri hend′
15. ô′ tə mā′ shən

Consonant Sounds: Exercise 15 (p. 47)
1. ə noun′ ser
2. sēz
3. dred′ fəl
4. un hap′ ē
5. wun′ dər fəl
6. trū′ ənt
7. grant
8. fo͞ot′ bol′
9. pēs
10. bi lēv′ ə bəl
11. kop′ ər
12. um brel′ ə
13. an′ ə məl
14. sok′ ər
15. reş′ ə pē

Consonant Sounds: Exercise 16 (p. 48)
1. **d**ock
2. **p**is**t**on
3. e**dit**
4. coa**st**al
5. **s**a**l**a**d**
6. **t**iger
7. **m**inor, **m**iner
8. **p**o**t**a**t**o

Consonant Sounds: Exercise 17 (p. 49)
1. plump

2. **m**an**d**ate
3. or**d**er
4. **n**igh**tl**y
5. **s**oaring
6. **h**al**t**
7. k**n**ock
8. **g**rape

Consonant Sounds: Exercise 18 (p. 50)
1. **c**able
2. **p**ig**g**y
3. **g**ra**v**y
4. **t**o**t**al
5. **n**o**str**il
6. **p**e**gb**oar**d**
7. **s**cru**ff**
8. **b**o**b**cat

Consonant Sounds: Exercise 19 (p. 52)
1. **g**iraffe
2. **j**u**dg**e
3. Ple**dg**e, Alle**g**iance
4. ur**g**ed, pro**j**ects
5. pa**j**amas
6. **g**enuine
7. **j**azz
8. privile**g**es
9. sub**j**ects
10. **j**ournal
11. **g**eraniums
12. stran**g**e
13. marria**g**es
14. fu**dg**e
15. **j**ewelry

Consonant Sounds: Exercise 20 (p. 53)
1. too**k**, sceni**c**, **c**ountry
2. pra**cti**cal
3. **C**an, **k**eep, se**c**ret
4. thin**k**, an**k**les
5. pa**ck**
6. **ch**ara**c**ter
7. ar**ch**ite**c**t
8. ju**k**ebox, musi**c**
9. **k**ey, **k**eyhole, lo**ck**
10. **c**ancel, ti**ck**ets
11. spe**c**tators

12. s**ch**olarship, **c**omputer, **c**amp
13. **c**ondu**c**tor
14. **c**ontinue, **c**onsume, **c**alories
15. **c**aterpillar, **c**o**c**oon

Consonant Sounds: Exercise 21 (p. 54)
1. the**s**e
2. **z**ing, pepper**s**
3. Plea**s**e, alphabeti**z**e, word**s**
4. **Z**oology, animal**s**
5. Mai**z**e
6. comedie**s**, **z**any, character**s**
7. sometime**s**, whee**z**e
8. Su**z**anne, u**s**ed, **z**oom, len**s**, picture**s**
9. belong**s**, tho**s**e
10. **z**ipper, Phil'**s**, un**z**ip
11. reali**z**e, million**s**, year**s**
12. **z**one
13. Who**s**e
14. sub**z**ero, tem-perature**s**
15. The**s**e, bar**s**, your**s**, tho**s**e, bar**s**

Consonant Sounds: Exercise 22 (p. 55)
1. fu**j**
2. kēp
3. sk**ō**ld
4. **j**ust
5. *thēz*
6. tik′ it
7. smu**j**
8. zō ol′ ə **j**ē
9. sok′ ər
10. plēz
11. chik′ ən
12. zip′ ər
13. *thōz*
14. **j**u**j**
15. sit′ ē

Consonant Sounds Review: Crossword (p. 56)

Consonant Sounds Review: Word Search (p. 57)
1. rain
2. storm
3. thunder
4. wind
5. tornado
6. hail
7. hurricane
8. lightning
9. ice
10. snow
11. sleet
12. drizzle

Word Search:

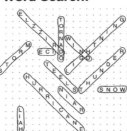

Vowel r Sounds: Exercise 1 (p. 59)
1. broth**er**, d**ir**t, de-liv**er**ed
2. b**ir**ds
3. n**ur**se
4. b**ur**lap
5. transf**err**ed
6. sunb**urn**, w**er**e
7. dess**er**t, sh**er**bet
8. C**ur**t, p**ur**chase
9. w**or**thy
10. m**er**c**ur**y

11. midt**er**m
12. h**er**bs
13. iceb**er**g
14. exc**er**pts, res**ear**ch, pap**er**
15. f**ir**mness

Vowel r Sounds: Exercise 2 (p. 60)
1. abs**or**bent
2. transp**or**t, f**or**ty-five
3. bookst**ore**
4. res**our**ces
5. cardb**oar**d
6. audit**or**ium
7. co**or**dination
8. C**or**ey, f**or**got, st**or**y, bef**ore**
9. fav**or**ite, c**or**n
10. f**or**ehead, do**or**
11. inf**or**med
12. b**oar**ds
13. perf**or**mance, perf**or**mer
14. **or**ganize
15. rec**or**der

Vowel r Sounds: Exercise 3 (p. 61)
1. f**ar**
2. **are**, superst**ar**s
3. **Ar**ctic
4. streetc**ar**
5. **ar**chery
6. sp**ar**kled
7. h**ar**d, **ar**tist
8. M**ar**ta, rhub**ar**b
9. C**ar**son, al**ar**m
10. p**ar**tner
11. c**ar**dboard
12. m**ar**sh
13. g**ar**ment
14. b**ar**becue
15. s**er**geant, **ar**my

Vower r Sounds: Exercise 4 (p. 62)
1. wôrn′ out′
2. ri zûrv′
3. ə sôr′ tid
4. kaf′ ə tîr′ ē ə
5. ə kûr′
6. wô′ tər mel′ ən

7. dan′ dər
8. bûr′ lap
9. si kûr′ ə tē
10. ri sûrch′, rē′ sûrch′
11. lēd′ ər
12. ôr′ thə don′ tist
13. un′ dər wô′ tər
14. shûr′ bit
15. härt

Vowel r Sounds:
Exercise 5 (p. 63)
1. har**r**den
2. bor**r**der
3. bi**r**thday
4. squi**r**t
5. gi**r**l
6. pa**r**tne**r**
7. sto**r**y
8. ga**r**den

Vowel r Sounds:
Exercise 6 (p. 64)
1. ca**r**nival
2. p**ar**t
3. pu**r**chase
4. pe**r**haps
5. b**ar**te**r**
6. sc**ar**e
7. tou**r**nament
8. **or**nament

Schwa Sound:
Exercise 1 (p. 66)
1. dī′ ət
2. ā′ pri kot, ap′ ri kot′
3. sel′ dəm
4. min′ it
5. op′ rə, op′ ər ə
6. fam′ ə lē
7. mī′ nəs
8. pol′ ish
9. prak′ ti kəl
10. deb′ ə när′
11. kôr′ rə spon′ dəns
12. prə pel′
13. ə rij′ ə nāt
14. bliz′ ərd
15. ā′ prən

Schwa Sound:
Exercise 2 (p. 67)
1. pā′ pər
2. thə, tē′ chər, thə, kwes′ chən

3. sev′ ən, ē′ kwəls, ē lev′ ən
4. thə, hwən, kwī′ ət
5. thə, fes′ tə vəl
6. mē′ dē əm
7. thə, in struk′ tər
8. thə, kem′ i kəls, sī′ əns, thə

Schwa Sound:
Exercise 3 (p. 68)
1. Thə, in′ fənt
2. thə, tā′ bəl
3. ə kā′ zhən
4. ā′ prən
5. lem′ ə nād′
6. win′ tər, bliz′ ərd
7. sten′ səl
8. pik′ əl, ham′ bûr′ gər

Other Sounds:
Exercise 1 (p. 70)
1. flaw
2. chalkboard
3. rainfall
4. alternate
5. fault
6. lawyer
7. oblong
8. nightfall
9. watermelon
10. salty
11. cloth
12. draw
13. Chocolate
14. officer
15. hauled

Other Sounds:
Exercise 2 (p. 71)
1. boyhood
2. subsoil
3. destroyed
4. hard-boiled
5. employed
6. joints
7. oil
8. joy
9. adjoining
10. toys
11. pointer
12. noise
13. ploy
14. toil
15. decoys

Other Sounds:
Exercise 3 (p. 72)
1. books
2. tour
3. poor
4. hood
5. took
6. brook
7. woodpecker
8. hoof
9. wool
10. nook
11. stood
12. looking
13. shook
14. cook
15. good

Other Sounds:
Exercise 4 (p. 73)
1. oozed
2. fool
3. too
4. moor
5. food
6. cool
7. brood
8. boots
9. hoop
10. root
11. noon
12. spoons
13. shoot
14. school
15. mood

Other Sounds:
Exercise 5 (p. 74)
1. outdoors
2. sound
3. rebound
4. amount
5. house
6. eyebrows
7. clouds
8. downhill
9. fountain
10. announce
11. drought
12. foul
13. crowd
14. drowning
15. chow

Other Sounds:
Exercise 6 (p. 75)
1. lŏŏk
2. toil
3. zōō
4. droun
5. wind′ fôl′
6. joi′ fəl
7. bŏŏk′ kās
8. fōōl′ prōōf′
9. flô
10. drout
11. our
12. härd′ boild′
13. en joi′
14. kôt
15. doun′ hil′

Other Sounds:
Exercise 7 (p. 76)
1. dispat**ch**ed
2. **ch**oke, **ch**erry
3. crou**ch**
4. **ch**ur**ch**
5. **ch**art
6. **ch**oose
7. **ch**ange
8. bat**ch**, **ch**ocolate, **ch**ip
9. **ch**eck
10. snat**ch**ed
11. **ch**eck, atta**ch**ed
12. mat**ch**
13. rea**ch**
14. pea**ch**
15. impea**ch**ed

Other Sounds:
Exercise 8 (p. 77)
1. **Wh**ere
2. **wh**ether
3. any**wh**ere
4. **wh**en
5. **wh**ich
6. **wh**innied
7. **wh**arf
8. **wh**eat, **wh**ite
9. **Wh**at, **wh**aling
10. **Wh**y
11. **wh**eeze, **wh**en
12. **Wh**ich, **wh**ey
13. **wh**eelbarrow
14. **wh**ack
15. **Wh**erever

Other Sounds:
Exercise 9 (p. 78)
1. sin**ging**
2. plan**ning**, Washin**g**ton
3. studyin**g**
4. ton**g**s
5. slan**g**, writin**g**
6. whistlin**g**, son**g**
7. pron**g**s
8. whisperin**g**, durin**g**, readin**g**
9. strin**g**, twan**g**
10. lan**g**uage
11. debatin**g**
12. wishin**g**
13. Lansin**g**
14. workin**g**, sprin**g**
15. goin**g**, meltin**g**

Other Sounds:
Exercise 10 (p. 79)
1. **Sh**e
2. fa**sh**ion
3. pu**sh**
4. **s**ure, **sh**ake, tra**sh**
5. bru**sh**
6. wi**sh**ing, wi**sh**es
7. **sh**abby
8. **sh**oes
9. **sh**ading, **sh**adows
10. **sh**eer
11. **sh**rubs
12. **sh**ack
13. **sh**ut, **sh**ow
14. **sh**rieked, **sh**uffleboard
15. pu**sh**, **sh**reds

Other Sounds:
Exercise 11 (p. 80)
1. **th**in
2. pa**th**
3. **th**umb
4. **th**reatened, **th**ought
5. **th**rown
6. E**th**er
7. my**th**s
8. heal**th**
9. leng**th**, wid**th**
10. **th**readbare
11. mon**th**

12. th**rottle**
13. **th**rough, **th**rough
14. wra**th**
15. **th**rone

Other Sounds:
Exercise 12 (p. 81)
1. **Th**at
2. ei**ther**, **the**
3. ba**th**ed
4. **the**
5. **Th**e, **the**, smoo**th**
6. bro**ther**
7. **Th**e, fea**th**ers, **the**
8. mo**th**er, fa**th**er, **the**
9. **th**at, **the**, **the**, praisewor**th**y
10. **th**ough, **the**
11. o**th**erwise
12. **Th**ese
13. **th**ey, **the**
14. ti**the**, **their**
15. ra**th**er, **th**an

Other Sounds:
Exercise 13 (p. 82)
1. *th*is
2. hwich
3. kach
4. pa**th**' wā'
5. fä' *th*ər
6. hüz
7. *th*at
8. brush
9. shrēk
10. wôsh
11. bring' ing
12. tē' chər
13. sông
14. mu*th*' ər
15. bā*th*

Accent Marks:
Exercise 1 (p. 84)
1. an' kle
2. cop' per smith'
3. sem' i co' lon
4. de served'
5. ter rain'
6. grand' stand'
7. man' a ger

8. pro jec' tion
9. out' spo' ken
10. pro pel'
11. mar' riage
12. in ves' ti ga' tion
13. mi' cro phone
14. caf' e ter' i a
15. farm' yard

Accent Marks:
Exercise 2 (p. 85)
1. pre vent'
2. ra' dar
3. de cide'
4. leop' ard
5. op po' nent
6. au di' tion
7. trop' i cal
8. thrust
9. im' pact
10. en gaged'
11. de fen' sive
12. tex' tile
13. cross' bar'
14. moun' tain
15. cru' cial

Accent Marks:
Exercise 3 (p. 86)
1. ē' *th*ər, ī' *th*ər
2. dē' fens, di fens'
3. tə mā' tō, tə mä' tō
4. kar' ə məl, kär' məl
5. rō' dē ō, rō dā' ō
6. pər' fikt, pər fekt'
7. min' it, mī nūt'
8. ri kôrd', rek' ərd
9. reb' əl, ri' bel
10. ri fūz', ref' ūs

Sentences will vary. Words with two different meanings are *perfect, minute, record, rebel,* and *refuse.*

Word Pronunciation
Review: Crossword
Puzzle (p. 87)

Word Pronunciation
Review: Word
Search (p. 88)
1. terrify
2. overwork
3. refund
4. pride
5. myth
6. idea
7. dollar
8. feet
9. basket
10. haste
11. confess
12. mine

Word Search:

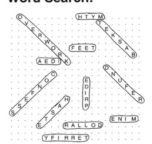

94